PK

MIDLOTHIAN LIBRARY SERVICE

Please return/renew this item by the last date shown. To
renew please give your borrower number. Renewal may
be made in person, online, or by post, e-mail or phone.
www.midlothian.gov.uk/library

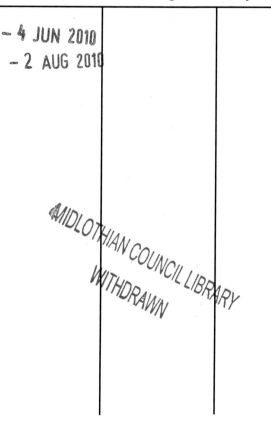

- 4 JUN 2010
- 2 AUG 2010

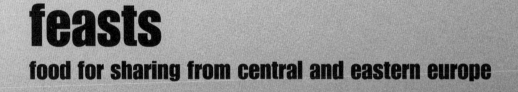

feasts
food for sharing from central and eastern europe

SILVENA ROWE

photographs by Jonathan Lovekin

For Malcolm, Illen and Alex, life's feast

Feasts: Food for Sharing from Central and Eastern Europe
by Silvena Rowe

First published in Great Britain in 2006 by Mitchell Beazley,
an imprint of Octopus Publishing Group Limited,
2–4 Heron Quays, London E14 4JP.
An Hachette UK Company
www.hachettelivre.co.uk

Reprinted 2006

First published in paperback in 2009

ISBN 978 1 84533 490 1

A CIP catalogue record for this book is available from the British Library.

Set in Trade Gothic and Impact

Printed and bound by Toppan Printing Company in China.

Commissioning Editor: Rebecca Spry
Executive Art Editor: Nicola Collings
Design: Caz Hildebrand
Editor: Susan Fleming
Photography: Jonathan Lovekin
Production: Jane Rogers
Index: John Noble

CONTENTS

INTRODUCTION

When you're in love, believe in it,
When you treaten, do not clown,
When you curse in the heat of the moment, do not back away,
When you are fighting, strike from the shoulder.

And when you argue, do it with a brave heart,
When you punish, carry it all out,
When you forgive, forgive with all your soul,
And when you feast, devour it all.

An unnamed poem by Aleksey Konstantinovich Tolstoy, *Complete Collected Poems – Volume 1*[1]

Eastern Europeans have a passion for food and life, and this manifests itself in a love of entertaining. Whether old friends or strangers, all are received with open arms and a full plate. Russians like to serve bread and salt, Bulgarians dried and smoked meats, and Poles beet soup and dumplings, but there is always one common theme: the welcome. And that is what this book celebrates. Here you'll find the subtleties and sophistication of little-known cuisines, superlative ingredients, often unfamiliar flavour combinations and, above all, a love of food shared by the countries of Eastern Europe – Russia, Bulgaria, the Czech Republic, Hungary, Poland and Ukraine among them.

Some people assume, perhaps due to the influence of the old Soviet Union, that the cuisine of Eastern Europe is one monotone whole, composed of bland, stodgy food eaten between bouts of vodka drinking. Nothing could be further from the truth. From the Baltic to the Black Sea, the landscape of Eastern and Central Europe is one of contrasts and beauty and, with its extremes of climate, it produces a variety of robust, honest foods that are rich in colour and flavour. The grains (such as wheat, corn and barley) and their products (such as dumplings, *mamaliga* and a multitude of breads), plus pulses (such as chickpeas), form the basics, which act as a backdrop to the flavourings, including vegetables and nuts such as beetroots, aubergines, walnuts and hazelnuts.

However, above all, the unique flavours of the area are provided by fruits, from the sour cherries and plums of the north to the pomegranates and apricots of the south, used both fresh and dried. These give a depth and balancing sweetness to many of the great dishes. Flavours are also provided by the subtle use of herbs and spices: dill, coriander seeds, marjoram, caraway, cumin and poppy seeds give an aromatically original depth to much of the food. All these ingredients survived the years of the Soviet Union, but it wasn't until the fall of the Iron Curtain that the richnesses of these Eastern European cuisines was introduced to the rest of the world.

The Russians, Czechs, Hungarians, Poles and Ukrainians are all rightly proud of their hearty, flavoursome dishes, which have changed little through the centuries. None of them has been immune to outside influences, though, in particular that of nineteenth-century French *haute cuisine,* which was imported by the Francophile nobility of the courts of St Petersburg in Russia. This gave us some classic Russian dishes: chicken Kiev, beef Stroganoff and veal Orloff, to name a few, were created for and named after their sponsors. Another influence comes from the Jewish Diaspora throughout eastern Europe, which was to create a culinary symbiosis with the cuisine of the host nations. I well remember, as a child, going to the Old Town in Plovdiv, in the south of Bulgaria, where you could eat the best of Jewish and Armenian food which was overlaid with Ottoman overtones. There, an elderly Jewish lady, Aunt Ester – known to everyone as Auntie (no-one knew her surname) – used to make the most marvellous *dolmeh* or stuffed vine-leaves. To this day, just the thought of them makes my mouth water. The cooking of the Balkan countries, from Serbia to Bulgaria, and along the Adriatic, formerly part of the Ottoman Empire, is noticeably spicier, with many flavours and textures showing the influences of Italy, Greece and Turkey.

At its heart, however, the Eastern European kitchen is country cooking at its best – robust and honest, but with a subtlety derived from the balancing of its strong but contrasting flavours. The soups vary from the hearty winter-warmers of Hungary to the sour soups of Poland to the light, delicate flavours of the summer-chilled soups that are common to the whole region and incorporate yoghurt and sour cream. The stews encompass the classic goulashes of Hungary, the sauerkraut-based dishes of Poland and Russia, and the aromatic braised lamb recipes of Georgia. The dumplings are legion, and include the classic *pierogi,* the delicate *uszka,* the savoury *leniwe* and the hearty *pyzy.* The subtle yet forceful marinades of central Asia, the pickling and preserving of the north, the smoked fish and caviar of Russia, the sausages and smoked meats, all play a big role in the kitchen. And these combine in a unique way to make the cuisine of Eastern Europe a rich and mostly unknown treasure trove that rivals the culinary cultures of France and Italy in depth and breadth.

Modern Eastern European cooking represents a *mélange* of the flavours of all these countries, using nuts, sweet and sour flavours and fruits in savoury cooking. Meat and vegetables are stewed with sour plums or pomegranates, sometimes with the sweeter quinces or prunes. Walnuts are not just a garnish but a vital component of a variety of dishes. Often yoghurt, pungent cheeses and wines are used to offset the richness of the nuts. The rich soil and the long, hot summers of the Balkan countries mean that local dishes use vegetables and fruits more commonly associated with the Mediterranean, such as courgettes, aubergines, tomatoes, apricots and peaches. Russian cooking, on the other hand, boasts rich soups and pancakes. Central European cooking reveals a legacy of the Austro-Hungarian Empire with its rich café culture and famous cakes and pastries, such as *Linzertorte* and *Dobos torte*. The aromatic cheese-filled breads and braised lamb dishes of Georgia have the pungency of Asia and the lightness of the Mediterranean.

I came early to an appreciation of my area's cooking. We lived, as did just about everyone, in an apartment block. Our neighbour was a widow, outside whose door I would hover, trying to catch a whiff of the smoky aromas of my favourite aubergine and walnut caviar, something I still make to this day. Bella Behar would occasionally bring some out to me, with a slice of sour rye bread with *schmaltz* and gherkins. She was amazed that a child could appreciate her cuisine, but for me it was the beginning of a long, rich and fascinating journey. A journey that led to this book.

fires of festivities
STARTERS AND SMALL BITES

When first the sunbeams Cancer fills

And the loud nightingale is still,

In Czarny Las from oldest days

Sobolka fire is wont to blaze

The neighbouring swain, the distant guest

Around the sacred fire have prest,

The orchards with the joyous sound

Of three gay fiddlers Laugh around.

Sobolka Fire by John Kochanowski, *Specimens of the Polish Poets*[2]

There is a long-standing tradition in Eastern Europe of welcoming guests into the home. The hardships of daily life are of little consequence. No matter how small the apartment (and they usually are very small), there is always room for a guest. The table is laid with a crisp white linen cloth and perhaps a vase of wild flowers, the best crockery and glassware are brought out of storage, and everything is set to welcome the visitor. Vodka, other spirits or wine will be offered and toasts proposed to health and prosperity. *Zakuski* (small *hors d'oeuvres*) will be served. *Zakuski* means literally a "mouthful to swallow with a drink", and this is the kind of food the Spanish call *tapas,* the Bulgarians and Turks *meze*, the Greek *mezes* and the Chinese *dim sum*.

The ritual of the starter table is one of the great pleasures of Eastern and Central European cuisine, its origins going back into the mists of time. It can be anything from a glistening display of ritzy dishes such as grey Beluga, velvety gold or tan Osetra or the bright red-orange salmon caviars, smoked and cured fish and pâtés through to more frugal vegetable caviars, pickled herring (*schmaltz*), salami-style sausages, cheeses and pastries.

One thing is for certain, though, as an old saying goes: "There is never enough food on the table, but always more than enough." In the West we write notes thanking our hosts for inviting us, but in Russia the host writes those notes to thank his or her guests for accepting the invitation. The saying "When a guest enters the home, God enters the home" or, as Pushkin would have it, the guest becomes a "holy person", unites people of all the countries of this region.

Blini

Makes 20-30 (depending on size)

This is my tried-and-tested recipe for *blini*. It makes delicate, light, fluffy *blini,* and no other recipe comes close. I like to use plain flour, but you can use buckwheat or rye flour instead if you wish. My secret is adding sour cream to the mixture, which makes the *blini* extra light and slightly plump. *Blini* cook very fast and you must always use butter to cook them in rather than oil, which would make them very heavy. They are best eaten just after cooking. With practice you will also improve your speed, so don't despair if it takes you a little time to cook them all at the beginning. Offer them as canapés topped with Beetroot and Date Caviar or *Gravadlax* (see pages 14 and 20).

160g (5³/₄oz) plain flour
160ml (5¹/₂fl oz) barely warm milk
10g (¹/₄oz) caster sugar
1 tsp salt

2 eggs, separated
10g (¹/₄oz) fresh yeast
1 tbsp sour cream
100g (3¹/₂oz) clarified butter

Place the flour in a large mixing bowl and make a well in the centre.

Add the sugar and salt to the milk, and mix well. Stir in the egg yolks and yeast, and mix until all is dissolved. Pour this into the well in the flour, then very slowly mix the flour with the liquid until everything is amalgamated and smooth. Leave covered in a warm place until the *blini* dough has doubled in size, about 1-2 hours.

Stir the sour cream into the dough. Whisk the egg whites to soft peaks and fold into the dough.

To cook, place a heavy non-stick frying pan on a high to medium heat and, using a pastry brush, brush its surface with some butter.

Using a dessertspoon, ladle spoonfuls of the dough, a few at a time, into the frying pan. Cook for 40 seconds, until golden brown, then flip over with a spatula and cook for another 40 seconds.

Serve with your favourite toppings (*see* suggestions in the recipe introduction) or simply with caviar.

Beetroot and Date Caviar

Serves 6

Beetroot is found on most menus in the cuisines of Russia, Poland, Georgia and Ukraine. Dates are among the best-loved dried fruits available during the long winters, storing the taste and warmth of summer. The Bulgarian Jewish community, now decreasing in numbers, has always thought of dates as a symbol of peace. This caviar can be offered with *blini* or as an accompaniment to a roast duck, pork or goose.

4 medium beetroots, washed and trimmed
5 plump dates, stoned and chopped
2 tbsp Cognac
4 garlic cloves, peeled and chopped
2 tbsp lemon juice

50g (1^3/$_4$oz) chopped walnuts
2 tbsp sour cream
salt and pepper
2 tbsp chopped fresh chives

Preheat the oven to 200°C/400°F/gas mark 6. Wrap the beetroots in foil and bake for about an hour. Meanwhile, put the dates in a heatproof bowl. In a small saucepan, heat the Cognac. Pour it over the dates, and leave them to soak for at least 30 minutes.

When the beetroots are cooked and cooled, peel them and chop the flesh coarsely. Place in a food processor with the dates, Cognac and garlic. Process until coarsely puréed.

Transfer to a mixing bowl and add the lemon juice, walnuts and sour cream. Mix and season with salt and pepper. Sprinkle with fresh chives.

Aubergine and Walnut Caviar

Serves 6

When I used to cook at *Books for Cooks*, I often made this caviar, and people always asked me for the recipe. In the Mediterranean it is known as aubergine caviar, and sometimes yoghurt, *tahini* or mayonnaise is added. The secret of this salad's success is the smoky flavour of the cooked aubergine. This is how my mother prepares it, and she in turn got the recipe from a family friend, Mr Hesim Nonhoff, who was the owner of the finest Jewish restaurant in Plovdiv (the town I come from). Serve the caviar with warm crusty bread. Sometimes I add a few seeds pomegranate seeds.

2 large aubergines
juice of 2 lemons
4 tbsp olive oil
4 garlic cloves, peeled and crushed

5 tbsp chopped fresh parsley
salt and pepper
50g (1³/₄oz) shelled walnuts, chopped

Pierce the aubergines with a long fork or skewer. Place them on the gas ring on a naked flame, and cook them like that, turning over, until the whole aubergine is char-grilled and soft. Alternatively, place them under a hot grill. Place the cooked aubergines in a colander and leave to cool. When they are cool enough to handle, peel off the blackened skin and discard. Gently squeeze the aubergines dry.

Chop the flesh into small pieces and place in a large bowl. Add the lemon juice, olive oil, garlic and parsley, and season to taste with salt and pepper. Mix well and adjust the seasoning. Add the chopped walnuts. Serve cold with pitta or any other flatbread.

Tahini and Walnut Caviar

Serves 6

Yet another delicious vegetable caviar with slight Middle Eastern influences. Serve with rye bread and crispy lettuce leaves. Tahini is not uncommon in the cuisines of Bulgaria, Russia and Georgia.

200g (7oz) shelled walnuts
3 garlic cloves, peeled and finely chopped
150g (5¹/₂oz) tahini

juice of 2 large lemons
salt and pepper
75ml (2¹/₂fl oz) water, or more if needed

Pan-roast the walnuts in a large heavy pan on a medium heat until golden brown, about 5 minutes. Cool and grind most of them in a food processor, reserving a few whole for decoration.

In a medium bowl, mix the garlic, tahini and lemon juice, and season to taste. The paste will be very thick at this stage, so add a little water and continue beating with a fork until you have the consistency of very thick double cream, adding more water as needed.

Add the ground walnuts to the tahini and refrigerate until ready to use. When ready to serve, sprinkle with the reserved whole walnuts.

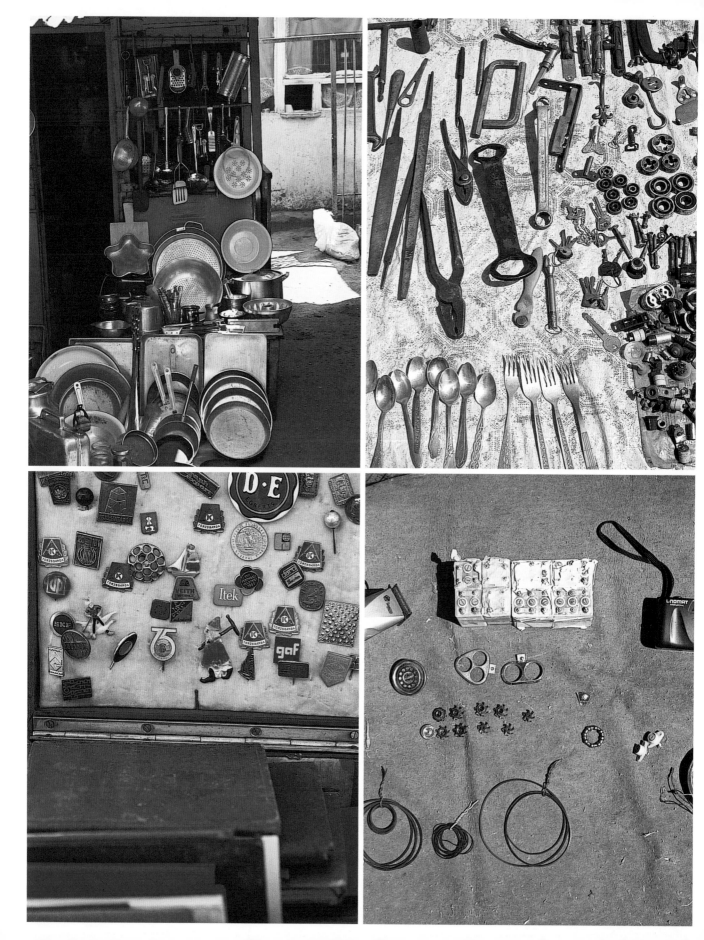

Roast Pumpkin Soup with Chestnuts and Walnuts

Serves 6

Pumpkins and chestnuts are two of the most exciting autumn foods, and although I am a carnivore, here is a temporary slip into vegetarianism. Both pumpkins and chestnuts have amazing texture, colour and structure, which together create a dramatic effect. The secret of this delicious soup is the slow roasting of the pumpkin to allow the full development of its flavour.

1.2kg (2lb 11oz) pumpkin, skin on, seeds removed, and cut into squares

4-6 tbsp olive oil

4 shallots, peeled and finely chopped

2 tbsp Marsala

120g (4^{1}/$_{2}$oz) chestnuts, skinned and chopped (from a tin is fine)

200ml (7fl oz) buttermilk

200ml (7fl oz) vegetable stock

1 tsp finely chopped fresh marjoram

1 tsp finely chopped fresh sage

100g (3^{1}/$_{2}$oz) shelled walnuts, toasted and coarsely chopped

Preheat the oven to 190ºC/375ºF/gas mark 5. Place the pumpkin in a roasting tray, coat with most of the olive oil, and bake for at least an hour. Cool and scoop the soft pumpkin flesh, together with any cooking juices, into a small container. Discard the skin.

In a medium saucepan heat the remaining oil and sauté the shallots until soft, about 2-3 minutes, on a medium heat. Add the Marsala and simmer on a low heat until almost all the liquid has evaporated. Add the chestnuts and sauté for a further 3 minutes.

Add the pumpkin flesh to the saucepan and remove from the heat, mixing well. Place the mixture in a food processor and purée until soft, adding some buttermilk and vegetable stock.

Place the soup back in the saucepan and add more buttermilk and stock to achieve the desired consistency. Cook on a slow heat for 10-15 minutes.

Add the herbs, and serve the soup hot, sprinkled with the walnuts.

Baked Filo Pastry with Feta and Honey

Makes about 20

Feta, my favourite cheese, is much used in the cuisines of Bulgaria, Poland and Russia. The most popular pastry is filo (or *phyllo*), and many housewives still prepare their own as a matter of pride. You can't beat home-made filo, but it is difficult and time-consuming to make. Luckily, filo is widely available in supermarkets and food shops, fresh or frozen, and this is fine. The combination of salty and sweet is as common as sweet and sour in these cuisines, and I remember as a child having this pastry hot, oozing with creamy feta, with lashings of velvety home-produced honey for breakfast.

250g (9oz) sheep's milk feta cheese, crumbled
200g (7oz) curd cheese
1 large egg yolk
1 tsp freshly ground black pepper
1 tsp freshly ground cumin seeds

20 sheets filo pastry
150g (5^1/$_2$oz) butter, melted
2 tbsp poppy seeds
5-6 tbsp clear honey

Preheat the oven to 180°C/350°F/gas mark 4. Combine the feta and curd cheeses in a bowl, and stir in the egg yolk, black pepper and cumin seeds.

Take a sheet of filo pastry and place it in front of you, making sure that the remaining pastry sheets are covered with a damp cloth; otherwise they will dry very fast. Lightly brush the sheet of filo with some melted butter and fold it in half lengthwise. Brush with butter and fold in half again.

Place some cheese mixture on the pastry along the shorter edge nearest to you, and roll the pastry over the filling away from you, rolling it to form a small Swiss roll, making sure that you are folding the sides of the pastry inwards at the same time to enclose the filling entirely. Do not roll too tightly as the filo will burst when baking. Continue in the same way with the rest of the filo sheets and cheese mixture, until both are used up.

Place the finished pastries on a baking tray and brush generously with melted butter. Sprinkle with poppy seeds and bake for about 20 minutes, until golden brown.

Serve warm with a little honey on the side.

Gravadlax
Beetroot, Dill and Vodka-Marinated Salmon

Serves 6

This is one of the easiest ways to make your own *gravadlax,* and the results are spectacular. Beetroot, dill and vodka are three very typical ingredients of the cuisines of Eastern Europe. The marinated salmon makes a wonderful first course when served as a topping on *blini* or just with crusty bread. The recipe is Russian, and was created originally for the Romanoff family. The touch of vodka is my addition.

1 x 400g (14oz) piece salmon fillet, scaled and bones removed
2 tbsp sea salt
2 tbsp granulated sugar
250g (9oz) raw beetroot, peeled and grated
finely grated zest of 1 orange
2 tbsp vodka
a large bunch of fresh dill, finely chopped

Garnish (optional)
beet or endive salad leaves
6 pink radishes, grated
2 shallots, peeled and finely sliced
a few fresh dill sprigs

Place the salmon on a chopping board with the skin facing down. Mix the salt and sugar and rub evenly over both sides of the fish.

In a small bowl, mix the grated beetroot, orange zest, vodka and chopped dill. Press the mixture all over the salmon. Wrap with clingfilm and then in foil, put on a plate, and place a weighted tray or plate on top of the salmon fillet. Chill for 36 hours.

After chilling, unwrap the fish. Remove the coating ingredients at this stage if you prefer, or simply slice the fillet and serve thin slices of the marinated salmon, discarding the coating.

If desired, garnish with beet or endive leaves, grated radish, finely sliced shallots and dill.

Croquettes à la Kiev with Horseradish Mayonnaise

Makes 20-25 (depending on size)

Croquettes are small savoury or sweet preparations, and are typically offered as a canapé or starter in the cuisines of countries such as Poland and Russia. Croquettes are made with veal, chicken, mushrooms, rice and various fish. They are called *kotletki*, and are a variation of the classic chicken cutlets *Pozharsky*, which is the original!

500g (1lb 2oz) salmon fillet, skinned/boned
2 slices white bread
100ml (3^{1}/$_{2}$fl oz) milk
1 large egg, beaten
2 tbsp finely chopped fresh dill
salt and pepper
150g (5^{1}/$_{2}$oz) butter
2-3 garlic cloves, peeled and crushed
200g (7oz) brioche breadcrumbs, toasted
vegetable oil, for shallow-frying

Horseradish Mayonnaise
200g (7oz) good-quality mayonnaise
2 tbsp sour cream
1 tsp French mustard
2 tbsp horseradish cream
1 tbsp fresh horseradish root, grated
2 tbsp lemon juice
^{1}/$_{2}$ tsp fennel seeds, finely ground

To make the horseradish mayonnaise, simply place all the ingredients in a large bowl and mix well. Adjust the flavours by adding more horseradish and/or lemon juice if you wish.

To make the croquettes, chop the fish finely. Soak the bread slices in the milk and squeeze almost dry of the surplus liquid. Chop the bread into small pieces. Place the salmon, bread, egg, dill and salt and pepper to taste in a food processor and process until smooth.

Using your fingers, shape the salmon mixture into small, walnut-like shapes and keep in the fridge, covered, until you are ready to cook. Meanwhile, mix the butter and garlic together and shape into small, hazelnut-like shapes, placing them in the fridge, covered, too. Leave to rest for about an hour.

Remove the fish and the butter from the fridge. Insert a garlic-butter ball into the centre of each salmon ball, making sure that you seal the hole well. Roll the salmon croquettes in the toasted brioche breadcrumbs and refrigerate until ready to use, for up to 2 hours.

Heat the oil in a large non-stick pan and cook the croquettes, a few at a time, turning so all sides are evenly coloured, about 3-4 minutes per side. Serve hot with the horseradish mayonnaise.

Kulebiaka
Salmon Pie

Serves 6

A classic Russian recipe, this is a rectangular pastry pie filled with layers of salmon, rice, wild mushrooms and eggs. The recipe below is my version, in which I use buckwheat instead of rice, which has slightly Polish undertones.

500g (1lb 2oz) fresh salmon fillet, skinned
  and boned
85g (3oz) butter
2 small shallots, peeled and finely chopped
200g (7oz) wild mushrooms, washed
  and dried
150g (5¹/2oz) buckwheat grains, boiled
  until tender

2 tbsp chopped fresh dill
2 tbsp lemon juice
salt and pepper
450g (1lb) fresh puff pastry
3 large eggs, hard-boiled, shelled and chopped
1 large egg, beaten

Preheat the oven to 180°C/350°F/gas mark 4. Cut the salmon into 5cm (2 inch) pieces.

Melt half the butter in a medium pan, and fry the shallots until soft, about 5-6 minutes. In another pan melt the remaining butter and sauté the mushrooms for a few minutes, until cooked. Cool slightly. Stir the cooked buckwheat into the shallots with the dill, lemon juice and some salt and pepper.

Roll out the puff pastry on a lightly floured surface to a 25-30cm (10-12 inch) square. Spoon the buckwheat mixture over half of the pastry, leaving 1cm (1/2 inch) around the edges. Arrange the salmon on top and sprinkle with the chopped hard-boiled egg. Top with the wild mushrooms.

Brush the edges of the pastry with the beaten egg and fold the pastry over the filling to make a rectangle, pressing the edges together. Brush liberally all over with the rest of the beaten egg and place the pastry on an oiled baking sheet.

Bake on the middle shelf of the oven for 30-40 minutes, until the pie is golden brown. Cool slightly before cutting to serve.

Smoked Salmon Potato Cakes with Garlic Cream

Serves 6

These easy cakes are made entirely with smoked salmon and potato, with no added flour. Use good-quality floury potatoes, which will help make the cakes light and fluffy. The garlic cream is a must. I usually roast large quantities of garlic and keep it in the fridge until needed.

450g (1lb) potatoes, peeled

300g (10^1/$_2$oz) smoked salmon, finely chopped

a small bunch of fresh parsley, finely chopped

4 spring onions, finely chopped

1 large egg, lightly beaten

150g (5^1/$_2$oz) fresh breadcrumbs, toasted

50g (1^3/$_4$oz) sesame seeds

5-6 tbsp olive oil

Garlic Cream

1 large garlic bulb, roasted

2 large egg yolks

juice of 1 large lemon

150ml (5fl oz) olive oil

salt and pepper

a small bunch of fresh dill, finely chopped

To make the garlic cream, squeeze the garlic out of each clove of the bulb, like squeezing toothpaste from a tube, into a food processor. Add the eggs and lemon juice. Add the olive oil gradually in a thin stream, with the motor running, until the mixture thickens. Season to taste with salt and pepper, and finish by adding the dill. Refrigerate until ready to use.

Cook the potatoes in boiling water until almost done. Cool and then grate them into a large bowl. Mix the smoked salmon, parsley, spring onions and egg into the potato. Season with salt and pepper.

Shape the mixture into 12 small cakes. Mix the breadcrumbs with the sesame seeds and coat the cakes evenly with them.

Place a large non-stick frying pan on a medium heat and add a little oil. Sauté the cakes until brown and cooked through, about 5 minutes on each side. Serve hot with some garlic cream.

Herrings with Sour Cream

Serves 6

The man in the wilderness asked me,
How many strawberries grow in the sea?
I answered him as I thought good,
As many as red herrings grow in the wood.

Traditional British rhyme

Herring is the most common fish in the cuisines of the Baltic countries and Poland, because it is fished in huge quantities in the Baltic Sea. It is eaten fresh or preserved as salted fillets, either *matjes* (pronounced "mat-jis"), which are less salty, or *schmaltz,* which are more salty. In the States, where herring was and still is considered a Jewish fish, it is an everyday staple food for most Eastern European Jewish emigrants. In New York, there are a lot of herring dealers concentrated in the Brooklyn area, where *matjes* and *schmaltz* herrings have been prepared since the 1930s.

400g (14oz) preserved herring fillets
¹/2 tsp French mustard
200ml (7fl oz) milk
salt and pepper
2 large shallots, peeled and finely chopped
200ml (7fl oz) sour cream

4 large hard-boiled eggs, shelled and
 finely chopped
a small bunch of fresh dill, finely chopped

Place the herring fillets in a shallow oval dish and pour in the milk. Cover and refrigerate for at least 4 hours.

When ready, remove and dry with kitchen towels. Discard the milk. Roll the fillets in spiral rolls and arrange on a large platter. Season with salt and pepper.

In a medium bowl, mix the chopped shallots, sour cream, mustard, boiled eggs and dill. Serve this with the herring rolls accompanied by some crusty brown bread.

Herring Pâté

Serves 6

An alternative recipe for preparing herring, which are widely available and inexpensive.

200g (7oz) fresh herring fillets, boned
50g (1³/₄oz) soft butter
1 tbsp horseradish cream
1 tsp sour cream
a pinch of caster sugar
freshly ground black pepper
2 small apples

To Serve
6 slices rye bread
1 small red onion, peeled and cut into rings
1 large apple, cored and sliced into rings,
    tossed in the juice of 1 lemon
50ml (2fl oz) sour cream
6 sprigs fresh parsley

Chop the herring fillets and place in a food processor with the butter, horseradish cream, sour cream, sugar and black pepper. Pulse on and off until the mixture is smooth but not minced.

Peel the apples and grate finely, adding them to the herring mixture. Mix well and refrigerate until ready to use.

To serve, spread the pâté on the rye bread, and top with the onion and apple rings. Finish with a small dollop of sour cream and a sprig of parsley.

Cauliflower Soup with Caviar

Serves 6

This makes a perfect, light first course, or it could be served in tiny glasses as a canapé. The soup is creamy and velvety, and it looks wonderful topped with some luxurious Sevruga caviar. If you are unable to obtain Sevruga, any fish caviar is fine to use instead.

10g (1/4oz) butter
1 shallot, peeled and finely sliced
1 medium cauliflower, cut into florets
500ml (18fl oz) milk

50ml (2fl oz) single cream
salt and pepper
100ml (3 1/2fl oz) crème fraîche (optional)
85g (3oz) Sevruga caviar

In a large saucepan, melt the butter and sweat the shallot to soften, about 5 minutes. Add the cauliflower florets and cook on a low-to-medium heat for a further 5 minutes.

Cover with the milk, bring to boiling point and then immediately reduce to a simmer. Put the lid on and continue to simmer for about 25 minutes, until the cauliflower is soft.

Blend the soup in a food processor, then return to the pan, add the single cream and some seasoning, and keep warm.

To serve, pour the soup into bowls and spoon on some crème fraîche, if using, with a spoonful of Sevruga on top.

Georgian Meatballs with Pine Nuts and Sour Cherries

Serves 6

These are delicious, nutty and very flavoursome meatballs, which contain both dried fruit and meat, a favourite marriage in the cuisines of Bulgaria, Georgia, Armenia and Hungary. I like my meat ground coarsely, so these meatballs are chunky. I first tasted this dish in Djvary, a small Jewish-Georgian restaurant in Tbilisi, where the owner, the delectable Mr Guledany, kindly let me have the recipe. The original was prepared with lamb and served with the most delicious *khachapuri* bread.

200g (7oz) ground veal
200g (7oz) ground chicken
1 onion, peeled and finely chopped
3 garlic cloves, peeled and crushed
50g (1³/₄oz) dried sour cherries, chopped
50g (1³/₄oz) pine nuts, roughly chopped and
  lightly toasted
¹/₂ tsp Hungarian paprika

¹/₈ tsp ground allspice
¹/₈ tsp powdered cinnamon
1 egg white, lightly whipped
a small bunch of fresh coriander, finely
  chopped
a small bunch of fresh mint, finely chopped
salt and pepper
2 tbsp vegetable oil

Combine the veal and chicken in a bowl, then add the onion, garlic, sour cherries, pine nuts, paprika, allspice and cinnamon. Mix well, then add the egg white and mix again. Finally, add the fresh herbs and salt and pepper to taste and mix thoroughly.

Shape the mixture into small balls the size of golf balls.

Heat the oil in a frying pan, then sauté the meatballs, a few at a time, turning occasionally, until cooked through and brown on all sides, about 10 minutes. Serve hot or at room temperature.

Vodka

Drinking vodka is a tradition in Russian and Poland. People drink to make even the smallest of occasions a celebration, to commemorate, to socialize, to cure an illness, to keep warm or to cool down. Vodka and *zakuski* are inseparable and often *zakuski* are known as "vodka-chasers". Vodka is more than a national drink today, it is drunk at all hours: in the morning to cure hangovers, at lunch to accompany a snack, and at dinner, when drinking vodka as a toast is a ritual.

    The word "vodka" in Russian means "little water". It is often drunk straight, but it can also be flavoured. Flavouring vodka is one of the oldest traditions in Russia, and everything from tree bark to fruit leaves, herbs and spices is used to infuse the spirit. Sour cherry, lemon or other fruit vodka infusions are particularly suitable for serving with fish, and are easy to make at home.

Lemongrass and Pink Peppercorn Vodka

Infuse 4 tsp pink peppercorns and 1 halved stick lemongrass in a 75cl bottle of vodka for at least 8 hours, but no longer than 2 days, depending on how hot and spicy you want it to be. Strain into a jug and pour back into the bottle. Store in the freezer and serve, almost frozen, in shot glasses.

Mixed Berry Vodka

Put in a large jug 100g each of fresh strawberries, raspberries, cherries and cranberries; 50g (1½oz) blackberries; 2 passionfruit, halved; 10 large sprigs fresh mint; and 2 tbsp clear honey. Add a 75cl bottle of vodka and let it stand, covered, for at least 3 days, then drain. Serve ice-cold with a few berries in each glass.

Cranberry Vodka

Crush 100g (3½oz) fresh or frozen cranberries and add them to a 75cl bottle of vodka, along with 1 tbsp clear honey. Infuse at room temperature for 24 hours and strain.

Zubrovka Buffalo Grass Vodka

Somerset Maugham, in his novel, *The Razor's Edge,* described buffalo-grass vodka as a drink that "smells of freshly mown hay and spring flowers". It is one of the most popular flavoured vodkas and perfect to accompany the venison dish on page 71. Buffalo grass is available from health and herb shops. Add 8 sprigs buffalo grass to a 75cl bottle of vodka and infuse for 6-8 hours. Remove 7 of the sprigs and leave just the 1 in the bottle. Chill and serve.

Lemon Vodka

Add the grated zest of 2 lemons to a 75cl bottle of vodka and infuse for 4 hours, but no more than 10, as the vodka will become bitter. Strain and chill.

Sour Cherry Vodka

Crush 50 cherries and their pits and add them to a 75cl bottle of vodka, along with 1 tbsp clear honey. Infuse at room temperature for 24 hours and strain.

apple of many seeds
SWEET AND SOUR

The Carthaginian garnet tinctured gemstones sparkle in their sacs,

Their succulence broken from leathery skin

That is princely blossom crowned,

And burst in tiny buds of mystical healing power,

Spreading their sweetness o'er the tongue.

Pomegranates by Malcolm J Rowe[3]

"Sweet and sour" is, without a doubt, the first answer that comes to mind to the frequently asked question, "What are the flavours of Eastern Europe's cuisines?". Here we find quinces, sour cherries, tart plums and crimson pomegranates used in savoury dishes.

Beetroot soups such as borscht feature in the cuisines of Poland, Russia and Ukraine, and it is believed that well over 100 recipes for borscht exist. The soup's sour tang can be intensified by the addition of tart apples, sauerkraut or prunes, and it is served with dumplings.

The sweet-and-sour flavours of the cuisines of Russia, Georgia, Armenia, Bulgaria and Poland are reminiscent of both Mediterranean and Middle Eastern tastes. Cooking fruits and meat together, in dishes such as braised duck with almond and pomegranate sauce, pomegranate and plum-glazed racks of lamb or braised lamb with prunes (*see* pages 38, 43 and 44) may reveal strong ties with the cuisines of Persia and Iran, but these dishes are nevertheless typical of their region. The Polish are particularly fond of sour cherries, the Bulgarians adore prunes in meat casseroles and use sauerkraut often, and the Georgians and Armenians favour pomegranates and plums.

The pomegranate, also known as "the apple of many seeds", is one of the most versatile fruits used in savoury cooking. Its ruby-like, juicy seeds are a perfect addition to summer salads, its tart juice works wonderfully when added to meats or salad dressings, and pomegranate molasses (a syrup made from the fruit itself) is ideal for marinades and adding to many dishes.

Sauerkraut (pickled cabbage) brings a distinctive sour taste to many Eastern European dishes . Every year, my mother made it (and still does). The cabbage would be chopped and placed in a large barrel, where in time it acquired a succulence and density of flavour from the fermentation process, with the help of some rock salt and another secret ingredient. Just as with borscht, many regions claim to make the best sauerkraut: from the former East Germany and Poland to Russia; not forgetting Bulgaria, of course.

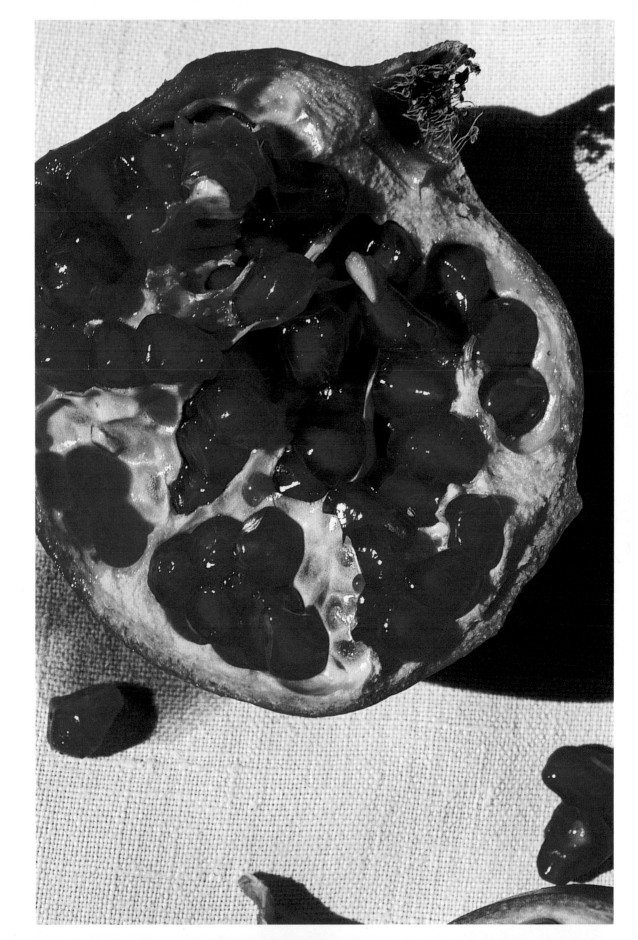

Borscht
Beetroot Soup

Serves 6

Borscht: the centre of everything!

Ukrainian proverb

There are two popular soups in Russia – *shchi* (a cabbage soup) and borscht. *Shchi* is the most common, and yet it is borscht that is better known around the world. Almost every household in Russia has its own version of borscht. Strictly speaking, borscht is a meat and beetroot soup, originating from Ukraine, and the recipe below was given to me by a Ukrainian.

1 x 400g (14oz) piece pork belly	4 medium beetroots, peeled and grated
15g (¹/₂oz) butter	250g (9oz) white cabbage, finely shredded
3 carrots, peeled and grated	1 sour green apple, peeled and grated
salt and pepper	1 large potato, peeled and grated
1 medium onion, peeled and finely chopped	200ml (7fl oz) sour cream (optional)

Place the pork belly in a large saucepan and cover with water. Bring to the boil, then reduce the heat and simmer for an hour, until the pork is cooked, skimming as necessary. Remove the pork and chop finely, then place back in the saucepan with the cooking liquid.

Meanwhile, in a large frying pan, melt about a third of the butter and sauté the carrots, seasoning with salt and pepper and stirring all the time. When the carrots have become translucent, add the onion and continue cooking for another 5 minutes. Remove the cooked carrot and onion to a large bowl. Add the remaining butter to the frying pan, along with the grated beetroots. Cook for 10 minutes, until the beetroots release their juices and their colour changes to deep purple.

Place the cooked carrots, onions and beetroot in the saucepan with the chopped pork and finally add the cabbage, apple and potato. Season to taste and add more water if needed, depending on the consistency you want (I usually add about 500ml of water at this stage). Bring to the boil and almost immediately reduce to a simmer. Continue simmering on a very low heat for at least 2 hours, uncovered, stirring occasionally. I like to simmer my borscht for at least 3-4 hours on the lowest heat. The colour is like nothing else, a deep crimson!

Just before serving, add a dollop of sour cream if desired.

Braised Duck with Almond and Pomegranate Sauce
Serves 4

My mum used freshly ground nuts in savoury sauces, so when on my travels in the region of the old Soviet Union I found that the republics of Georgia and Azerbaijan had many dishes that used almonds and walnuts in their sauces, I wasn't surprised. The presence of nuts gives a particular texture and body to the sauce and it makes it rather delicious. The mellow, milky almonds and sweet-and-sour flavours of the pomegranates create the perfect company for the slightly gamey flavours of the duck. This is best served with a rice pilaff. Pomegranates are increasingly available in supermarkets, so obtaining some shouldn't be difficult.

1 large duck, about 2kg (4lb 8oz)
2 tsp olive oil
1 large Spanish onion, peeled and chopped
$^1/_2$ tsp ground turmeric
$^1/_2$ tsp ground cumin
250ml (9fl oz) chicken stock
300g (10$^1/_2$oz) ground almonds

500ml (18fl oz) pomegranate juice, about 5-6 large pomegranates or bottled juice
4 tbsp lemon juice
1 tsp caster sugar
$^1/_2$ tsp ground cardamom
salt and pepper

First of all prepare the duck. Quarter it, rinse it well and dry it thoroughly with paper towels.

Heat the oil in a large non-stick casserole dish, and brown the duck pieces on all sides, a few at a time. Remove the duck and keep warm.

Now add the onion to the casserole dish, and sauté for a few minutes in the duck fat, stirring over a medium heat. Add the turmeric and cumin and cook for a further 5 minutes. Add the chicken stock and bring to the boil. Turn down to a simmer, then add the almonds and pomegranate juice, and continue simmering for another 20 minutes. Stir in the lemon juice, sugar and cardamom, and season to taste.

Now return the duck quarters to the casserole, cover, and cook on a medium heat for at least 1$^1/_2$ hours, or until the duck is cooked. Serve hot.

Dill and Mustard-Stuffed Chicken

Serves 4

This recipe is a *mélange* of delicious flavours, inspired by memories from my childhood, and enriched by recent travels to research this book. The combination of dill and mustard is very exciting. Serve with mustard greens.

1.5kg (3lb 5oz) free-range chicken,
  ready to cook
3 tsp mustard-seed oil

Stuffing
a small knob of butter
1 shallot, peeled and finely chopped

4 tbsp blanched almonds, chopped
100g (3^1/$_2$oz) dried sour cherries
100ml (3^1/$_2$fl oz) dry white wine
2 slices white bread, whizzed into
  breadcrumbs
2 tsp grain mustard
a small bunch of fresh dill, finely chopped

Preheat the oven to 200°C/400°F/gas mark 6.

To make the stuffing, melt the butter in a medium saucepan and cook the shallot and almonds over a low heat for 3 minutes, until the shallot is soft. Add the cherries and wine, and cook until the wine has almost evaporated. Stir in the breadcrumbs, mustard and dill, mixing well. Season to taste.

Spoon the filling into the cavity of the chicken, then place in a roasting tray. Brush the mustard-seed oil all over the chicken.

Roast for 30 minutes, then reduce the temperature to 180°C/350°F/gas mark 4 and continue cooking for another hour, basting every now and again with the cooking juices.

To check if the chicken is cooked, pierce the thickest part of the bird with a skewer and if the juices that run out are clear the bird is done. Keep in a warm place until ready to serve.

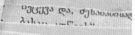

Pomegranate, Pumpkin and Lamb Stew

Serves 4

Eugene Lobzhanidze now lives in London, but her maternal grandparents left Gori in Georgia (also known as the birthplace of Stalin) for Miami in Florida around the turn of the twentieth century. She remembers her grandmother making this dish, which was popular in the East European Jewish community in their Florida neighbourhood. Lamb and pomegranates are perfect together, and this is a wonderfully fruity one-pot dish for winter. I use lamb shoulder, the flavour of which I find sweeter than that of the more expensive leg. It is difficult to identify the exact origins of this dish, but lamb and pomegranates are cooked together in the regions of Georgia and Armenia. I had a similar dish in a Georgian restaurant in Moscow.

3 tbsp olive oil
1 x medium lamb shoulder, boned and cut
   into 3cm (1^1/$_4$ inch) pieces
salt and pepper
1 large onion, peeled and finely sliced
2 garlic cloves, peeled and crushed
1 large sweet red pepper, chopped

^{1}/$_2$ tsp ground cumin
a pinch of dried chilli flakes
350ml (12fl oz) lamb stock
3 tbsp pomegranate molasses
400g (14oz) peeled pumpkin, chopped
a small bunch of fresh coriander, finely
   chopped

Heat the oil in a large casserole dish and add the diced lamb. Stirring constantly, cook until the meat is evenly browned on all sides. Season with salt and pepper. Transfer the meat to a plate.

Add the onion, garlic, pepper, cumin and chilli flakes to the casserole dish and cook, stirring, for a minute or so. Return the lamb to the dish and add the stock and pomegranate molasses. Bring to the boil, then reduce the heat, cover, and simmer for about an hour on low heat.

Add the pumpkin and cook for a further 20 minutes, until the pumpkin is very soft and the lamb is cooked through. I like to cook it for longer than that, until the pumpkin is completely mushy.

Add the coriander and serve hot with cooked pearl barley or rice.

Pomegranate and Plum-glazed Racks of Lamb

Serves 4

The combination of the slightly sour and tart pomegranate and the tender lamb is delicious, a dish inspired by my travels in Georgia.

2 racks of lamb, French-cut
salt and pepper

Pomegranate and Plum Paste
4 large ripe plums, stoned and chopped
3 tbsp pomegranate molasses
2 garlic cloves, peeled and crushed
2 tsp chopped fresh rosemary
2 tbsp olive oil

For the paste, place the plums in a food processor and process until puréed. In a medium bowl, stir together the pomegranate molasses, plum purée, garlic, rosemary and oil. Mix well.

Coat the racks with two-thirds of the paste and leave, covered, for an hour or so in the fridge.

Meanwhile, preheat the oven to 200°C/400°F/gas mark 6.

Place the coated racks of lamb in a large roasting dish, season with salt and pepper and cook in the oven for 20 minutes. Baste every now and again with the remaining paste. The lamb should be cooked to medium-rare; cook longer for well-done.

Transfer to a cooling tray and let stand, loosely covered, for about 5 minutes. Cut in individual pieces and serve with pilaff.

Braised Lamb with Prunes

Serves 6

In Bulgaria, prunes have a wonderfully smoky flavour. Dried fruits are used a lot in the winter, when fresh seasonal fruit is not available. This recipe was, and still is, a regular on our weekly family menu. My mum's friend Adi Aharon used to cook this dish using the finest kosher chicken, as chicken was a lot cheaper than lamb. Prunes are especially popular in the Jewish-Hungarian kitchen (sweet-and-sour tastes are very common in Jewish Eastern European cooking). I find that the lamb is complemented beautifully by the subtle sweetness of the prunes.

5 tbsp vegetable oil

1 large onion, peeled and finely chopped

600g (1lb 5oz) boned leg of lamb, cut into
5cm (2 inch) cubes (keep bones for stock)

2 tbsp plain flour

salt and pepper

200ml (7fl oz) stock from the lamb bones

1 tbsp caster sugar

5 tbsp white wine vinegar

2 bay leaves

1/2 tsp powdered cinnamon

pinch of ground cloves

200g (7oz) prunes, stoned

a few sprigs of parsley, finely chopped

Heat the oil in a casserole dish, add the onion and sauté until lightly coloured. Meanwhile, dust the meat with flour, salt and pepper and add it to the casserole. Cook until the meat is browned. Add the stock and simmer until the sauce has slightly thickened, about 20-30 minutes.

Add the sugar, vinegar, bay leaves, cinnamon, cloves and prunes. Bring to a boil, and then simmer again for about 20 more minutes, until the meat is tender. Serve while hot, sprinkled with parsley, with either some rice or boiled potatoes.

Papricas
Veal and Paprika Stew with Sour Cream

Serves 4-6

Papricas, pronounced "papricash", is another traditional stew typical of Hungary, but it is also cooked in Romania and Bulgaria. *Papricas* is made always with lean meat – veal, chicken or rabbit – and cooked with sour cream. *Papricas* is my favourite stew, and this recipe is one that has been well tried and tested.

1 medium onion, peeled and chopped

3 tbsp vegetable oil

1 tsp sweet (noble) paprika

600g (1lb 5oz) veal shoulder, cut into
    3cm (1¹/₄ inch) cubes

100ml (3¹/₂fl oz) water

2 large tomatoes, cubed

salt and pepper

2 green sweet peppers, seeded and
    thinly sliced

400ml (14fl oz) sour cream

2 tsp plain flour (optional)

Sauté the onion in the oil in a heavy based saucepan until just golden.

Remove from the heat and add the paprika, stirring well (if you add the paprika on the heat, it will burn and become bitter). Place back on the heat, and add the meat, water and tomatoes. Season with salt and pepper, mix, cover and cook for 15 minutes, adding a little more water if necessary.

Remove the lid and continue cooking on a low heat for 15 minutes longer. Add the sliced green peppers and stir well.

Combine two-thirds of the sour cream with the flour, if using, and add to the sauce. Cook on a low heat for 5-7 more minutes; the veal should be cooked through. Serve the stew hot with a dollop of the remaining sour cream.

Golabki
Stuffed Cabbage Leaves
Serves 6

This is a deliciously rich, meaty, smoky recipe for stuffed cabbage leaves. It was given to me by my Polish friend Robert, whose mother prepares it almost weekly back home in Poland.

1 whole medium Savoy cabbage
6 bay leaves

Stuffing
1 large onion, peeled and finely chopped
vegetable oil
100g (3½oz) *cabanos* sausage, sliced

100g (3½oz) Polish smoked sausage, sliced
150g (5½oz) plain white rice
250g (9oz) veal or pork mince
a small bunch of fresh parsley, finely chopped
3 tbsp finely chopped fresh oregano
3 tbsp tomato purée
salt and pepper

Wash the cabbage and cut out the hard core, taking care not to break the leaves. Put the cabbage in a large, deep saucepan with enough water to cover it. Slowly bring it to the boil, then reduce it to a simmer for at least 30-40 minutes, depending on the size of the cabbage; the cabbage is cooked when it has got paler. Drain and cool. Break off the leaves and place them on a work surface.

Preheat the oven to 180°C/350°F/gas mark 4. For the stuffing, cook the onion in 2 tbsp oil in a frying pan until golden, about 10 minutes. Place in a large mixing bowl. In the same pan, heat a further 2 tbsp oil, and gently cook the sliced sausages for 10 minutes on a medium heat, until they are evenly browned. When they have cooled, chop them finely and add them to the bowl.

In a large saucepan, heat a further 2 tbsp oil, then add the rice. Cook on a high heat until the rice granules are browned, about 5 minutes or so, stirring constantly. This will not only cook the rice but give it a wonderfully smoky flavour. Add the rice to the cooked onion and sausage.

Add the remaining filling ingredients to the bowl, season, and mix well. Using your hands, make small sausage shapes of the mixture and place each on the middle of a whole cabbage leaf. Fold the nearest end to you over the filling, then the two sides, and finally the part furthest from you. Place the stuffed leaf in a roasting tray, seam-side down. Repeat with all of the other whole cabbage leaves. If any leaves are broken, do not use to wrap, but leave to one side.

Add about 4 tbsp water to the roasting tray and arrange the bay leaves on top, finally covering all the cabbage rolls with the broken leaves. Cook for 50 minutes, then increase the heat to 200°C/400°F/gas mark 6, and cook for a further 10 minutes.

Sweet Feta and Almond Vine-leaf Parcels with Orange and Rose-water Syrup

Serves 6

In Bulgaria, vine leaves are precious and can be used in many ways. There are grapevines all over the country and almost every country house has its own vine. When I arrived in London 20 years ago, the realization that I would not be able to get hold of fresh vine leaves came as a shock to me, as up to that point they had been a vital ingredient in my everyday diet! Still, I found a small vine in my neighbours' back garden and to their amazement I asked for leaves to cook with. Today you can get jars of vine leaves in almost every deli, as well as major supermarkets.

My father used to prepare the recipe below, which was given to him by his friend Sarkis Zaken (the best and most inspired Jewish pastry chef in my town) before he emigrated to Brighton Beach in New York, where he opened his own pastry shop. It is a wonderful summer pudding, the fragrant and crunchy vine leaves stuffed with mellow, creamy feta and milky and satiny almonds. The syrup... well, you just have to take my word for it. The flavour of rose-water is subtle and typical of Bulgaria, which is famous for its endless valleys of roses.

250g (9oz) sheep's milk feta cheese, cubed
50g (1³/₄oz) shelled whole almonds,
    toasted and slightly crushed
1 tbsp ground almonds
1 tsp caster sugar
12 large fresh or preserved vine leaves
seeds of 1 large pomegranate

Orange and Rosewater Syrup
50g (1³/₄oz) caster sugar
1 cinnamon stick
1 orange, thickly sliced
2 tsp rose-water

To make the orange and rose-water syrup, place all the ingredients except the rose-water in a saucepan together with 400ml water. Bring to the boil, then simmer for 30 minutes until the liquid has thickened and its texture has become syrupy. Cool and then stir in the rose-water.

In a medium bowl, place the feta, ground almonds, most of the crushed almonds and the sugar and mix well with a fork.

If using fresh vine leaves, blanch in boiling water for 1-2 minutes. Place a vine leaf flat on a work surface in front of you and scoop a large tbsp of the feta mixture into the centre, folding the leaf over the bottom and sides to cover the feta. Repeat with the rest of the leaves and feta mixture.

Place all the vine parcels in a shallow dish, and sprinkle with the pomegranate seeds. Pour in the syrup generously, and refrigerate until ready to serve.

Apple Strudel

Serves 6

Making a strudel pastry is a dying art. In the depth of the Hungarian countryside, housewives still make their own filo, but ready-made is the next-best thing. A true strudel should be fine, crisp and light, with very thin pastry filled with fruit. Apple is the most common filling, but you can also use cherries or savoury fillings such as sauerkraut.

60g (2^1/4oz) butter, melted, plus extra

500g (1lb 2oz) cooking apples, peeled,
    cored and cubed

1 tbsp lemon juice

75g (2^3/4oz) shelled pecans, roughly chopped

85g (3oz) caster sugar, plus extra

35g (1^1/4oz) brioche breadcrumbs

10 large sheets fresh filo pastry

icing sugar to decorate

Preheat the oven to 200°C/400°F/gas mark 6. Butter and line a flat baking tray.

Place the apples and lemon juice in a medium saucepan and cook over a medium heat for around 5 minutes, until the apples are soft.

In a bowl mix the apples, nuts, sugar and breadcrumbs.

Lay out a damp cloth on a work surface and place a sheet of filo pastry on it. Brush generously with melted butter, then cover with another sheet of filo, brushing again with butter. Repeat the process with the rest of the sheets.

Once you have all the filo buttered and stacked in front of you, place the apple and pecan mixture in the middle of it and roll up the pastry like a Swiss roll.

Butter the roll on all sides, sprinkle on some extra caster sugar. Place on the prepared tray and bake for 20-30 minutes, until golden brown.

Please note that the picture is of 4 individual strudel rolls prepared in Hungary by village women, and uses homemade filo pastry. Your strudel will not look exactly like this.

Cherry and Pistachio Gratin

Serves 6

The cherry season in Eastern Europe is something else. The cherries are luscious, juicy and plump. Here in the UK, cherries are a luxury, and when not in season they are imported from the USA, France or Turkey; if we are able to afford them at all, we would buy them by the ounce. The recipe below is easy and has within it some Ottoman touches: for instance, the pistachios, which grow in abundance in Turkey. This Ottoman culinary influence is still very vivid in countries such as Bulgaria, Poland, Croatia and Hungary, and adds a certain exoticism to the cooking of those countries. This recipe is from Carmel Pince, possibly the best Jewish restaurant in Budapest.

100g (3^1/$_2$oz) shelled pistachios, crushed
50g (1^3/$_4$oz) brioche breadcrumbs
50g (1^3/$_4$oz) light soft brown sugar
1 tsp vanilla extract

150ml (5fl oz) double cream
2 large eggs
2 tsp melted butter
500g (1lb 2oz) cherries, washed and stoned

Preheat the oven to 200°C/400°F/gas mark 6.

Place the pistachios, brioche breadcrumbs, sugar, vanilla, cream and eggs in a food processor and blend until combined.

Lightly butter a medium-sized square baking tin and place the cherries in one layer on its base. Pour in the gratin mixture.

Bake for 30 minutes. Serve warm accompanied by plain thick yoghurt.

Fresh Berry Pavlovas

Serves 4-6

This dessert is a favourite all over the world, but few people know its origin. It was named after the Russian ballerina, Anna Pavlova, in honour of her graceful performance of the dying swan, when she visited Australia in 1929. A pavlova with fresh berries is a classic. It consists simply of a crisp-on-the-outside, chewy-on-the-inside meringue, accompanied by the fragrant wild berries found in abundance in the Baltic countries. Summer here arrives later than in the rest of Europe, but the berries it brings are special and well worth waiting for. Berry and fruit tarts, berry soups and custard, and berry desserts are common in countries like Estonia, Lithuania and Latvia, and berry picking is a favourite national pastime.

5 egg whites
300g (10^1/$_2$oz) caster sugar
2 tsp cornflour
1 tsp white-wine vinegar

300ml (10fl oz) double cream, whipped
500g (1lb 2oz) mixed fresh berries (wild strawberries, raspberries, blueberries)

Preheat the oven to 180°C/350°F/gas mark 4. Lightly oil a large flat tray and line it with non-stick baking paper.

Beat the egg whites until thick with shiny peaks. Beat in the sugar a little at a time, then beat in the cornflour and vinegar. Do not over-mix.

Make 4-6 large meringues by scooping dollops of the egg white on to the lined tray. Don't worry about them looking uniformly shaped.

Place the meringue tray in the oven and immediately turn the temperature down to 150°C/300°F/gas mark 2. Cook the meringues for about 50 minutes without opening the door. When cooked, they should be a pale honey colour. Turn off the oven and let the meringues cool completely before removing them.

To serve, spoon some whipped cream on to each pavlova and spoon some mixed berries on top.

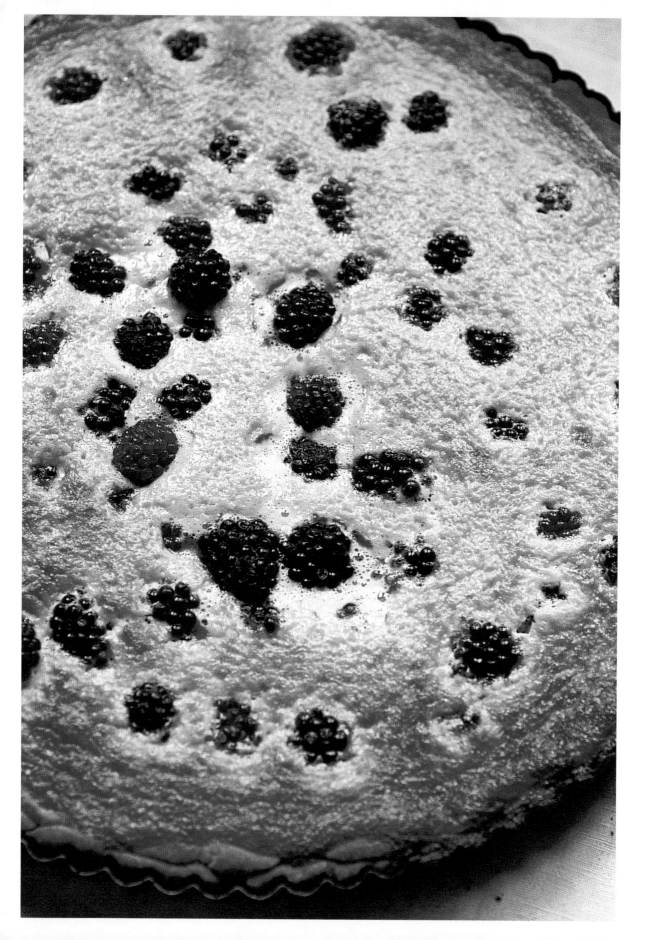

Blackberry and Buttermilk Tart

Serves 8

Buttermilk is a slightly sour liquid, made by separating the butter fat from the cream after churning it. It has a tangy flavour and is widely used in many countries in Eastern Europe, especially Russia and the Baltic countries, for breads or desserts. This tart is best made when the berry season is in full swing, but you can substitute other fruits when fresh berries are not available.

225g (8oz) plain flour
50g (1³/₄oz) caster sugar
115g (4oz) unsalted butter, chopped
¹/₄ tsp almond essence

Buttermilk filling
2 large egg yolks
1 whole egg
70g (2¹/₂oz) soft brown sugar
50g (1³/₄oz) vanilla sugar
seeds from 1 plump vanilla pod
1 tsp cornflour
250ml (9fl oz) buttermilk
50ml (2fl oz) double cream
500g (1lb 2oz) blackberries

Place the flour and sugar in a food processor and combine well. Add the butter and pulse in short bursts until the mixture resembles breadcrumbs. Add the almond essence and some water, if needed, for the pastry to come together.

Place the pastry dough in front of you on a floured work surface and knead gently. Wrap in clingfilm and place in the fridge for an hour.

When ready, roll out the pastry on a floured surface until 4mm thick, and use it to line a tart dish of about 22-24cm (8-10 inches) in diameter. Cover and place in the fridge for an hour.

Preheat the oven to 180°C/350°F/gas mark 4. Line the tart shell with baking paper and fill it with baking weights or dried beans or other pulses you may have in the cupboard (and keep specially for this purpose). Blind-bake for 15 minutes. Remove the paper and weights and bake for a further 5 minutes, until lightly browned.

To make the filling, whisk together the egg yolks, egg, sugar, vanilla sugar, vanilla seeds and flour. Gently heat the buttermilk and double cream together, and gently whisk into the egg mixture.

Place the blackberries in the tart shell and very carefully pour in the warm buttermilk mixture. Place in the oven, having reduced the heat to 160°C/325°F/gas mark 3, and bake for 35-40 minutes, until the buttermilk filling is firm.

Chocolate Cakes with Cherry Filling

Serves 6

I like to use brioche or milk bread for this recipe, but any light and fluffy bread will do. It is so easy to make and the combination of cherry and chocolate is perfect and unpredictable!

85g (3oz) dried sour cherries

2 tbsp cassis

2 tbsp caster sugar

1/2 tsp almond extract

100ml (3 1/2 fl oz) double cream

100g (3 1/2 oz) chocolate, 70% cocoa solids

40g (1 1/2 oz) soft butter

1 large brioche

Preheat the oven to 180°C/350°F/gas mark 4.

Place the cherries, cassis and sugar in a small saucepan and bring to the boil. Stir in the almond extract. Let it stand for 10 minutes to cool. In another saucepan, heat the cream and chocolate together over a low heat until the chocolate has melted. Remove from the heat and add a third of the butter and the cherries with their liquid, and stir. Pour into a plastic bowl and place in the fridge for at least 2 hours, until the mixture has become a solid mass.

Cut the brioche into slices, about 1cm (1/2 inch) in thickness. Cut 12 rounds with a small round cutter (about the size of the bottom of a ramekin dish) and also cut 24 rectangles from the remains of the slices. Butter all the brioche cuttings with the remaining butter and arrange 6 rounds, buttered-side down, on the bottom of 6 ramekin dishes. Line the sides with the rectangular pieces, 2 per dish, buttered side on to the ramekin dish itself. Make sure that you overlap the rectangular pieces slightly so there are no gaps.

Spoon the filling evenly into each of the 6 dishes and top each with the remaining rounds, buttered-side up. Press down gently.

Bake for 20-25 minutes, or until the brioche is golden brown. Cool slightly, invert on to serving plates, and serve warm.

Chilled Strawberry Soup

Serves 6

This is a typical Eastern European fruit soup. If you're lucky enough to taste a chilled fruit soup while visiting any of the countries in the Baltic triangle, you may stumble upon a wild strawberry or wild blueberry soup, which have very delicate, tart flavours. Blackcurrants, peaches and cherries can also be used to make cooling summer soups. The long, cold winters of Eastern Europe may require hearty, slow-cooked, warming stews, but then there are the hot, long summer months.

450g (1lb) ripe strawberries, hulled and washed
150ml (5fl oz) buttermilk

250ml (9fl oz) sour cream
2 tbsp fresh lemon juice, if needed

Place the strawberries in a food processor and purée. Press through a sieve and stir in the buttermilk and sour cream. Taste and, if desired, add a little lemon juice for a sourer taste.

Quince and Orange Curd

Fills 4 x 250-300ml (9-10fl oz) jars

The quince, also known as the "golden apple" or "love apple", is a fruit many of us are afraid to use. Greenish yellow in colour, it resembles a large apple, and has the sweetest perfume, similar to the aroma of pineapple and guava. Its flesh is ecru in colour and hard, which makes it difficult to eat raw. The quince is cooked slowly so that the flesh softens and becomes reddish in colour; then the seductive aroma of the quince is unrivalled. This curd recipe is perfect for tart and cake fillings, and can be stored in the fridge until needed. I offer it as a topping on crispy, light meringues.

1kg (2lb 4oz) quinces
200ml (7fl oz) water
400g (14oz) caster sugar
1 vanilla pod, split open

juice and finely grated zest of 2 oranges
100g (3$^{1}/_{2}$oz) unsalted butter
6 large egg yolks, beaten

Peel and chop the quinces and place them in a saucepan with the water, sugar and vanilla pod and its seeds. Simmer on a low heat until the quinces begin to change colour to pinkish red.

Remove the vanilla pod and pour the mixture in a food processor to purée until smooth. Return the quince purée to the saucepan and add the orange juice and zest, butter and eggs. Cook, stirring constantly, on a low heat until the mixture thickens.

When the curd is ready and cooled, pour into sterilized jars and seal to store in the refrigerator.

Pomegranate, Vanilla and Blood-Orange Sorbet

Serves 4-6

The colour of this sorbet alone is a good enough reason for making it! The sweet-and-sour flavour has a refreshing and cleansing effect and it makes the perfect finale to a feast. I like to squeeze my own pomegranate juice, but using shop-bought juice is the next-best thing.

100ml (3^{1}/$_{2}$fl oz) water
1 plump vanilla pod, split and seeds reserved
175g (6oz) caster sugar

450ml (16fl oz) pomegranate juice
225ml (8fl oz) blood orange juice
a handful of pomegranate seeds

Place the water, vanilla pod (not the seeds) and sugar together in a saucepan and stir over a medium heat until the sugar has dissolved. Cool.

Mix together the pomegranate juice, vanilla seeds and blood-orange juice, and add the water and sugar mixture, having removed the vanilla pod.

Transfer the sorbet mixture to an ice-cream machine and freeze for 20 minutes with the motor running. Remove the sorbet and place in a container in the freezer until needed. Serve sprinkled with pomegranate seeds.

MARINADES, GLAZES AND SAUCES

So when the first bold vessel dared the seas,

High on the stern the Thracian raised his strain,

While Argo saw her kindred trees

Descend from Pelion to the main.

Transported demigods stood round,

And men grew heroes at the sound.

Ode for Music on St Cecilia's Day by Alexander Pope,
Poetical Works – 2 Volumes[4]

Although many dishes don't require sauces – indeed, sauces can distract from the quality of a dish – sauces can also turn an ordinary recipe into something divine. As a small child, I remember my father transforming what I considered to be uninspired dishes into mini masterpieces merely by adding a delicate sauce.

The craft of preparing sauces, marinades and dressings is a great skill, but many housewives and cooks in countries such as Poland, Russia, Bulgaria, Hungary and Georgia have a special knack. And so the recipes in this chapter are all about the art of using marinades, making light and delicate sauces, and creating fruity and zesty dressings. Olive oil is a rarity here, unlike in the cuisines of France, Spain and Italy. Instead, sour fruits and tart pomegranate molasses are favoured, together with honey, pomegranate juices, verjuice and vinegars. Try pomegranate and plum-glazed racks of lamb for a tangy marinade (*see* page 43), or the delicious horseradish and sour cream dressing of the Estonian haddock salad (*see* page 67). The Polish simply couldn't live without the use of sour cream in their sauces (added to herrings, it is magic), and Bulgarians use yoghurt liberally as a main component in their salad dressings.

White Bean and Barley Salad with Beetroot and Yoghurt Dressing

Serves 4

Pulses and grains form an indispensable part of the cuisines of countries like Bulgaria, Hungary, and Poland. Rich in protein, carbohydrate and minerals, they are commonly used in everyday dishes, mainly soups and stews. For this recipe you may use any dried white beans you can find, such as butter-beans or haricots (soaked and cooked first) or canned beans.

1 x 400g can white beans, rinsed and drained
200g (7oz) cooked barley (just boiled)
50g (1³/₄oz) sultanas
2 tbsp chopped fresh parsley
2 tbsp chopped fresh thyme
50g (1³/₄oz) shelled walnuts, roughly chopped
salt and pepper
200g (7oz) baby salad leaves

Beetroot and Yoghurt Dressing
3 beetroots, washed
2 garlic cloves, peeled and crushed
250ml (9fl oz) thick yoghurt
35g (1¹/₄oz) ground walnuts

For this sauce, cook the beetroots in boiling water for about 20 minutes, until soft. Cool, then peel and place the flesh in a food processor with the garlic and yoghurt. Pulse until it is smooth and creamy. Pour into a bowl and stir in the ground walnuts.

In a large bowl, combine the beans, barley, sultanas, herbs and walnuts and mix well. Season to taste. Add the salad leaves and toss everything together gently.

Serve accompanied by the beetroot and yoghurt sauce.

Baby Spinach and Asparagus Tart with Pomegranate Molasses Dressing

Serves 6

Pomegranate molasses is versatile, and delicious when used to create fruity and zesty salad dressings – adding that unique sweet-and-sour twist. In essence it is a syrup made from the juice of the scarlet fruits. My Mum made her own pomegranate syrup every year around September when the new crop was ready, and we would drink it or use it as a condiment with salads or meats during the long winter days in my native Bulgaria.

200g (7oz) baby spinach, chopped
2 eggs
125ml (4fl oz) double cream
1 bunch new season asparagus, trimmed
   and washed
salt and pepper
3 tbsp freshly grated Parmesan

Pastry
225g (8oz) plain flour, plus extra for dusting
75g (2³/₄oz) chilled butter, cubed
a pinch of salt
50ml (2fl oz) milk
1 egg yolk

Pomegranate Molasses Dressing
2 tbsp pomegranate molasses
2 tbsp lemon juice
20ml (³/₄fl oz) olive oil

To make the pastry, put the flour, butter and salt in a food processor and pulse until crumbly. Add the milk and egg yolk and pulse until a dough forms. Turn out the dough on to a lightly floured surface and knead for a few minutes, then wrap in clingfilm and chill for at least 1 hour. Roll out the pasty on the floured surface to fit a greased 20 x 8cm (8 x 3 inch) rectangular tart tin. Chill for 20 minutes.

To make the dressing, combine all the ingredients and keep refrigerated until needed.

Preheat the oven to 180°C/350°F/gas mark 4. Line the tart shell with baking paper and place in it some baking weights or just dried beans, then blind-bake for 10 minutes. Remove the weights and paper, and bake the tart shell for a further 10 minutes, until it is golden brown.

Meanwhile, place the baby spinach in a saucepan with a few drops of water and cook over a high heat for 3-4 minutes, until wilted. Drain well and chop finely. Put the eggs, cream and spinach in a bowl. Mix well and season to taste with salt and pepper.

Lay the asparagus tips along the length of the tart shell next to each other, then pour the egg mixture over them. Sprinkle with the cheese and bake for 30 minutes, until golden brown. Serve the tart in slices with a crisp salad, and drizzle some pomegranate dressing over both.

Estonian Smoked Haddock Salad with Horseradish and Sour Cream Dressing

Serves 6

This zesty, light, summery dish has some unexpected flavours. Its meaty haddock chunks are beautifully dressed in a cool, silky horseradish sauce. Traditionally herrings would be used in this dish, but the method of preparation is still the same. Poaching rather than frying fish is the preferred way of cooking in the Baltic.

800g (1lb 12oz) smoked haddock fillet
2 tbsp lemon juice
1 cucumber
200g (7oz) baby spinach leaves, washed

Horseradish and Sour Cream Dressing
2 tsp horseradish cream
1 tsp freshly grated fresh horseradish
150ml (5fl oz) sour cream
1 tbsp mayonnaise
4 spring onions, finely chopped
a small bunch of fresh dill, finely chopped
salt and pepper

Place the smoked haddock in a shallow saucepan and just cover with water. Bring to the boil and simmer for 4 minutes, until cooked. Drain and, when the fish is cool enough to handle, remove and discard the skin. Break gently into chunky flakes and sprinkle with lemon juice.

To make the salad dressing, combine the horseradish cream and grated fresh horseradish, the sour cream, mayonnaise, spring onions and dill. Season with salt and pepper.

Cut the cucumber in half lengthwise, remove its seeds, then slice each half in thin slivers.

In a large mixing bowl, gently combine the fish, cucumber, spinach leaves and dressing. Serve immediately, while the fish is juicy and the salad leaves are crunchy.

Marinated Herring with Cucumber and Dill Salad

Serves 6

This is a wonderful example of sweet-and-sour flavours, and a good way of marinating and preparing herring. The salad is made in a similar way in Poland, Russia and Hungary, especially amongst the Jewish communities. (In Hungary they serve it as an accompaniment to *papricas, see* page 97.) This recipe relates most closely to the Polish salad version called *mizeria*, which means "misery" in Latin. Legend has it that Queen Bona Sforza adored this salad and couldn't get enough of it. The reason the salad was called *mizeria* is because the queen cried from homesickness for her native Italy while eating it.

60ml (2^1/4fl oz) white-wine vinegar

8 black peppercorns, crushed

2 bay leaves

4 allspice berries, crushed

2 cloves, crushed

^{1}/4 tsp yellow mustard seeds

1 shallot, peeled and finely chopped

1 tsp small capers, rinsed and chopped

1 tbsp chopped fresh rosemary

1 tbsp chopped fresh thyme

200g (7oz) herring fillets in oil, drained

Cucumber and Dill Salad

1 large cucumber

^{1}/2 tsp salt

juice of ^{1}/2 lemon

100ml (3^1/2fl oz) sour cream

2 tbsp finely chopped fresh dill

To prepare the marinated herring, mix together the vinegar, peppercorns, bay leaves, allspice berries, cloves, mustard seeds, shallot, capers, rosemary and thyme. Place the herring fillets in a large shallow dish and cover them with the marinade. Cover and refrigerate for a week.

The secret of the cucumber salad is to peel and slice the cucumber very finely. Place the slices in a sieve and sprinkle it with the salt, leaving it for 30 minutes or so to drain. The cucumber slices must be rinsed of excess salt and then dried. Place in a medium bowl with the lemon juice, sour cream and dill and mix well. Serve at once to accompany the marinated herring.

Venison with Juniper Berries and Sour-Cherry Sauce

Serves 6

Hunting has always been a passion for the Slavic people, and they take great pride in preparing intensely flavoured game dishes. Here, the robust venison contrasts nicely with the sweet-and-sour sauce. The meat is prepared with a marinade and rubbed with juniper.

6 x 150g (5^1/$_4$oz) venison medallions, tied with butcher's string
4 tbsp grape-seed oil
salt and pepper

Marinade	*Sour Cherry Sauce*
200ml (7fl oz) red wine	**20g (^{3}/$_4$oz) butter**
4-6 sprigs fresh thyme	**300g (10^1/$_2$oz) fresh or frozen cherries, stoned**
4-6 sprigs fresh rosemary	**2 tsp redcurrant jelly**
1 garlic clove, peeled and crushed	**^{1}/$_2$ tsp chopped fresh thyme**
1 small shallot, peeled and finely chopped	**100ml (3^1/$_2$fl oz) veal or good chicken stock**
1 small carrot, peeled and finely chopped	
1 celery stalk, finely chopped	
8 white peppercorns	
10 juniper berries, crushed	

Place all the marinade ingredients in a large container. Mix well and add the venison medallions to marinate overnight.

Preheat the oven to 200°C/400°F/gas mark 6.

When ready to cook the venison, remove from the marinade (reserving this) and dry well. Lightly brush the meat with some of the grape-seed oil, and season with salt and pepper. Seal the mini joints in a sauté pan in the rest of the oil, caramelizing on all sides. Place in the oven for 10-12 minutes for just pink, or longer if you like it medium to well-done. Slice the medallions in 3 horizontally when ready to serve.

To make the sauce, drain the vegetables from the marinade, reserving the liquid. Melt the butter in a heavy pan and sauté the marinated vegetables. Add the cherries, redcurrant jelly, thyme, half of the marinade liquor and the stock. Cook to reduce by half, then pass through a fine sieve, and season. Keep warm.

To serve, arrange the slices of venison on serving plates, and pour on the sour-cherry sauce. Offer buffalo-grass vodka (*see* page 31) with it.

Chicken with Grapes and Apricots

Serves 6

While working at Books for Cooks, this recipe was a favourite and I was always asked to make it. The tender, soft flesh of the chicken absorbs the delicate, slightly sweet flavours of the grapes and apricots. If apricots aren't in season, use dried ones instead.

1 large chicken, 1.8kg (4lb), cut into 8	*Marinade*
3 tbsp olive oil	1 tbsp clear honey
1 onion, peeled and chopped	1 tsp grated fresh root ginger
1 cinnamon stick	1 tsp powdered cinnamon
100g (3^1/$_2$oz) fresh seedless grapes, halved	1 tsp freshly ground black pepper
100g (3^1/$_2$oz) fresh apricots, halved and stoned	100ml (3^1/$_2$fl oz) white wine

For the marinade, in a large bowl mix together the honey, ginger, cinnamon, pepper and wine, and stir. Rub the marinade all over the chicken, cover and leave in the fridge overnight. Drain, reserving the liquid.

Heat the olive oil in a large sauté pan and sauté the onion until just golden. Add the chicken and brown all the pieces evenly, turning them. Add the chicken marinade and cinnamon stick and simmer for 40 minutes – the liquid should reduce by half.

Add the grape and apricot halves, and simmer, lid on for a further 5-8 minutes, until the chicken is cooked through. Remove the cinnamon stick and serve hot.

Pork Tenderloin with Beetroot and Mustard Sauce

Serves 4

Pork is a great favourite in countries such as Poland, the Czech Republic and Slovakia. The flavours of beetroot and mustard work well with the pork tenderloin. You could use pork chops instead.

15g (¹/₂oz) butter
1 x 400g (14oz) pork tenderloin
3 tbsp finely chopped fresh dill

Beetroot and Mustard Sauce
200ml (7fl oz) strong chicken stock
150ml (5fl oz) white grape juice
2 tbsp Dijon mustard
salt and pepper
2 large beetroots, cooked (*see* page 14)
   peeled and grated
1 tbsp pomegranate molasses
1 Granny Smith apple, peeled and grated

Preheat the oven to 180°C/350°F/gas mark 4.

In a heavy sauté pan, melt the butter and sauté the pork tenderloin, turning around to brown on all sides evenly. Cover with foil, transfer to the oven, and cook for 20 minutes, until cooked through. Keep warm.

Place the stock, grape juice and mustard in a saucepan and bring to the boil. Cook until reduced by half, then season to taste. Add any cooking juices from the pork along with the grated beetroot and pomegranate molasses, and continue cooking for a further 10 minutes to reduce further. The sauce will also thicken. Finally add the grated apple and heat through.

Slice the pork tenderloin and serve with the sauce poured over it. Sprinkle with fresh dill.

Veal and Quince Stew

Serves 6

The quinces in this stew are not going to change their colour to red, as sugar has not been added, but they will require at least 40 minutes' cooking to become tender. This dish has some Hungarian and Armenian roots and origins. It's delicious eaten the day after preparation.

1kg (2lb 4oz) veal shoulder, boned and cubed
1 large onion, peeled and chopped
vegetable oil
3 garlic cloves, peeled and crushed
$^1/_4$ tsp saffron strands
$^1/_2$ tsp sweet paprika
$^1/_2$ tsp ground cumin
200ml (7fl oz) veal stock
2 quinces
100g (3$^1/_4$oz) dried sour cherries
salt and pepper

Marinade
8 juniper berries, crushed
3 garlic cloves, peeled and crushed
1 cinnamon stick
200ml (7fl oz) dry red wine

Place the marinade ingredients in a large bowl. Add the veal, cover, and marinate in the fridge for 24 hours. Drain the meat when ready to use, and reserve the marinade.

Sauté the onion slowly in some vegetable oil in a heavy casserole dish for a few minutes. Add the garlic, saffron, paprika and cumin. Cook until the onions have softened, about 5 minutes.

Add the veal in batches to the onions, and cook until all the cubes are slightly browned on all sides. Pour in the reserved marinade and the veal stock, cover, and simmer for about an hour.

Preheat the oven to 180°C/350°F/gas mark 4.

Peel and core the quinces, and cut them into wedges. Add the quince and dried cherries to the stew, cover and stew in the oven for 45-60 minutes.

When ready, season with salt and pepper and serve hot.

Oxtail Stuffed with Mamaliga

Serves 4-6

Polenta (cornmeal) was the mainstay of diets in many south-eastern European countries as it was often a cheaper and tastier substitute for traditional grains. It became a staple for the Jews in Romania, where it was known as *mamaliga* and considered almost a national dish.

2 whole oxtails, chopped in segments
20g (³/₄oz) butter
1 x 300g can chopped tomatoes
600ml (1 pint) strong chicken stock
zest and juice of 1 large orange

Marinade
800ml (27fl oz) red wine
1 red onion, peeled and chopped
1 carrot, peeled and chopped
1 celery stalk, trimmed and chopped
2 garlic cloves, peeled and crushed
2 sprigs fresh thyme

Mamaliga Stuffing
300ml (10fl oz) milk, plus extra if needed
100g (3¹/₂oz) cornmeal
salt and pepper
50g (1³/₄oz) butter
100g (3¹/₂oz) Cheddar, grated

Mix all the marinade ingredients in a large bowl and add the oxtail pieces, making sure that they are all covered by the marinade. Cover and refrigerate overnight.

Preheat the oven to 180°C/350°F/gas mark 4.

Remove the meat from the marinade. Heat the butter in a large, heavy non-stick pan and briefly brown all the oxtail pieces. Reserving the liquid of the marinade, add the marinated vegetables and herbs to the oxtail and cover. Continue to brown for 5-8 minutes. Add the tomatoes, stock and orange zest and juice as well as the reserved marinade liquid. Cook in the oven for 2 hours.

To make the *mamaliga* stuffing, bring the milk to the boil and pour the in cornmeal all at once. Season and stir constantly to avoid lumps. The cornmeal will thicken as it absorbs all the liquid; add more if needed. The consistency should be rather thick, similar to that of wet polenta. This will take about 15-20 minutes. Add the butter and cheese, and keep warm.

When the oxtail is cooked, remove from the oven and cool slightly. Using a slotted spoon, lift and remove the pieces from the saucepan and carefully remove the centre bones from each of the oxtail pieces. Discard the bones. Using a small spoon, spoon some *mamaliga* into the middle of each of the circular oxtail pieces.

Serve 2-3 oxtail pieces per portion, accompanied by some sauce and vegetables.

Honey-Vodka Marinated Beef Fillet with Mustard Sauce

Serves 4

If you like carpaccio, then you must try this recipe. It was given to me by the chef at Austeria, a Jewish restaurant in Krakow, where I enjoyed it together with nostalgic music and Yiddish songs.

350g (12oz) freshest free-range beef fillet
coarse sea salt
a handful of rocket leaves

Marinade
3 tbsp vodka
$1/2$ tbsp clear honey
2 tbsp red wine
1 tbsp olive oil
2 tbsp black peppercorns, crushed
1 tsp allspice berries, crushed
2 tbsp chopped fresh chives
2 tbsp chopped fresh parsley
1 tbsp caraway seeds, toasted and ground

Mustard Sauce
1 egg yolk
3 tbsp Dijon mustard
7 tbsp sunflower oil
a big pinch of salt
a pinch of caster sugar
$1/2$ tbsp Tabasco sauce
$1/4$ tbsp Worcestershire sauce

Trim the meat of all sinews and excess fat. Combine the marinade ingredients and coat the meat evenly. Wrap tightly in clingfilm and refrigerate for 24-48 hours.

For the sauce, whisk together the egg yolk and mustard, then add the oil slowly to make a mayonnaise. Add the salt, sugar and sauces.

To serve, unwrap the beef and wipe off the marinade, then slice the meat as thinly as possible. Arrange on the plate and sprinkle lightly with coarse sea salt.

Garnish with a few rocket leaves and drizzle with the sauce. Some crumbled, home made croûtons add a pleasant additional crunch, but are not essential.

Balsamic-Roasted Pears with Honey

Serves 4

I had this dish on my last visit to Budapest, and for me it represents the combination of traditional and modern cooking, something that is becoming more and more evident on the culinary scene in Hungary. The caramelized balsamic flavours work beautifully with the sweet intonations of the pears and honey.

2 large slightly under ripe pears
2 tbsp butter

3 tbsp balsamic vinegar
4 tbsp clear honey

Preheat the oven to 200°C/400°F/gas mark 6.

Halve and core the pears but do not peel them.

Melt the butter in a heavy and non-stick ovenproof pan. When just beginning to bubble, add the pears, cut-sides down. Sauté for 2 minutes, then place the pan in the oven to roast the pears for 20 minutes.

Add the vinegar and roast for a further 5 minutes. Drizzle with honey and remove the pan from the oven, allowing the pears to rest. Serve warm.

Almond and Lemon Cake with Pomegranate Syrup

Serves 8-10

Old recipes for almond cakes have travelled around the world with the Jews since Ottoman times. The one thing that all these recipes have in common is the presence of sweet, milky almonds, matzo meal, sugar, eggs and lemons or oranges. The syrup in this cake is made with fresh pomegranate juice and honey. The cake tastes as stunning as its looks, topped with jewel-like, glistening pomegranate seeds. My mother made this cake only for special occasions and always with our home-grown almonds.

1 large lemon
150g (5^1/$_2$oz) butter, cubed, plus extra
350g (12oz) ground almonds
300g (10^1/$_2$oz) caster sugar
115g (4oz) plain flour
1 tsp baking powder
6 eggs
2 pomegranates, seeds only

Syrup
juice of 3-4 pomegranates, or 250ml (9fl oz) fresh bought pomegranate juice
4 tbsp clear honey
1 tbsp pomegranate molasses

To make the syrup, place the ingredients in a saucepan and stir well over a medium heat until the honey has dissolved. Continue cooking, stirring, until the liquid has reduced to two-thirds and has a syrupy consistency; about 10-12 minutes.

Meanwhile, place the whole lemon in a small pan, cover with water and boil for 25 minutes, until the skin is soft. Remove and cool. When cool enough to handle, place the whole lemon in a food processor and process to a purée, skin and all. Keep aside until needed.

Preheat the oven to 180°C/350°F/gas mark 4. Grease a 15cm (6 inch) square baking tin with extra butter, and line with parchment paper.

Place the ground almonds, half the sugar, plus the flour and baking powder in a large mixing bowl and mix well.

Beat the remaining sugar with the butter cubes until light and creamy. Add the eggs one by one, beating well in between. Add the puréed lemon and mix well. Gradually fold in the almond mixture and pour this into the buttered and lined baking tin.

Bake for 50-60 minutes. Test to see if it's fully cooked by inserting a skewer – if the skewer comes out clean, then the cake is ready; if not, bake it for a little longer.

When the cake has cooled slightly, turn it out of the tin on to a rack to cool completely.

Using a skewer, make deep holes in the top of the cake and slowly pour over the syrup, which will soak into the cake. Pile the pomegranate seeds on top.

the essence of taste
SPICES, SEEDS AND HERBS

The bigos *has been served! No verse can tell the splendour of its flavour, colour and smell. Sheer poetry and rhymes are mere pleasing sounds, whose sense no hungry stomach truly comprehends.*

Pan Taduesz by Adam Mickiewicz[5]

Seeds, spices and herbs bring together some of the otherwise very diverse cuisines of Eastern Europe. One of the most common spices is paprika, or "red gold" as the Hungarians call it (in the Slavic languages it is referred to as *piperka*. Paprika is synonymous with Hungary, but it is widely believed (at least by Bulgarians) that it was brought to Hungary by the Bulgarians. There are six categories of paprika, but the most frequently used in everyday cooking are noble (or sweet) paprika and hot paprika. Paprikas are graded according to piquancy, fineness and colour.

Famed for its use in the Hungarian goulash or *gulyas*, this fruity, powerful spice is one of the prime flavours of the region as a whole, with dishes given variety by the addition of the immense range of other spices blended with it. The traditional Hungarian *gulyas* is actually a soup rather than a stew and, historically, it was cooked in iron kettles over open fires by both herdsman and farmers. Made with paprika and caraway seeds, it was never thickened with flour into a stew-like consistency.

Cumin and caraway seeds are also common flavourings of the region, caraway used for its cooling and digestive effect, cumin used with meat and in stews. Marjoram is a favourite in Poland and is used year-round, fresh when it is available or dried when it is not. White borscht would be unthinkable without the use of dried marjoram. In Georgia, marigold (also known as Imertian saffron) and barberry seeds are used in many dishes. Meals are cooked simply but flavoured intensely with fresh herbs or dry spices.

Poppy seeds are used in baking – in strudels, biscuits and cakes – as are cardamom, cinnamon and cloves, spices that have come from the influences of the Ottoman kitchen.

Gyuvech
Vegetable Stew
Serves 6-8

Gyuvech is one of my father's specialties, a midsummer medley of seasonal vegetables, and he cooks it at least once a week when all the ingredients are in season. This famous dish originates from Turkey and, just as with goulash, it has many versions with subtle differences. It is popular in Romania, Hungary, Croatia and Bulgaria. The Turkish word *gyuvech* means a special earthenware pot in which vegetables are baked.

1 aubergine, cubed
salt and pepper
6 tbsp olive oil
3 courgettes, sliced into rounds
2 red onions, peeled and cut into eighths

150g (5^{1}/$_{2}$oz) okra, trimmed
400g (14oz) fresh tomatoes, cubed
1 red pepper, seeded and cut into squares
2 tsp sweet (noble) paprika
a large bunch of fresh parsley, chopped

Put the aubergine cubes in a colander, sprinkle with salt, and leave for 2-3 hours, letting the aubergine drain off excess liquid. Rinse and drain them.

Preheat the oven to 190ºC/375ºF/gas mark 5.

Heat 2 tbsp of the olive oil in a heavy frying pan and sauté the aubergine cubes and courgette slices for 3-4 minutes, until browned.

Put the remaining oil in a large earthenware dish and place in the hot oven for 5 minutes. When the oil is hot, take the dish out and add the onions, okra, tomatoes, pepper, aubergine and courgette. Sprinkle with paprika and season with salt and pepper. Stir gently to coat all the vegetables with oil and paprika. Return the dish to the oven and bake for an hour.

Add the parsley, and serve the stew hot, accompanied by crusty bread and yoghurt or, if you wish, sour cream as they do in Hungary.

Chicken Croquettes Stuffed with Pine Nuts and Dried Cranberries

Serves 4

These light, delicious croquettes were inspired by a dish I had a few years ago in a Jewish restaurant in Moscow called Zimes. If you can't get hold of dried cranberries, then use sultanas or dried cherries instead.

2 medium slices white bread	1 small onion, peeled and finely chopped
100ml (3^1/$_2$fl oz) milk	100g (3^1/$_2$oz) pine nuts
500g (1lb 2oz) chicken breast, minced	100g (3^1/$_2$oz) dried cranberries
5 tbsp finely chopped fresh parsley	^{1}/$_4$ tsp ground cumin
1 large egg	^{1}/$_4$ tsp ground cinnamon
salt and pepper	200g (7oz) brioche breadcrumbs
vegetable oil	

Preheat the oven to 180°C/350°F/gas mark 4.

Soak the bread in the milk for 5 minutes. Gently squeeze out the excess milk, and break the bread into small pieces. Put in a medium bowl, add the chicken mince, parsley and egg, and season with salt and pepper. Mix well.

To make the stuffing, heat 2 tbsp of the oil in a large frying pan and sauté the onion for 3 minutes. Add the pine nuts and allow them to gently brown, then add the cranberries, cumin and cinnamon and simmer gently for another 5 minutes. Remove from the heat.

Take a small handful – about 1 tbsp – of the chicken mixture and form into a flat disc. Place a tbsp of the pine-nut stuffing in the centre and wrap the edges around it, rolling it into a largish meatball. Gently form an oval croquette. Repeat with the remaining chicken mixture and stuffing.

Roll the croquettes in the fresh breadcrumbs and fry gently in some oil to brown, about 3 minutes on each side. Finish the cooking in the oven for 15 minutes, until cooked through. Serve hot.

Fricassee of Chicken and Olives

Serves 4

Apart from my father's fricassee, the best one that you could eat can be sampled in Shalom Kosher Restaurant in the Jewish quarter in Budapest. Fricassee is a light and fragrant stew, yet comforting and satisfying at the same time. Although originally French, it is also a very Eastern European dish, and I was brought up on it. The secret of a light and creamy fricassee is the fluffy sauce.

1 x 1.5kg (3lb 5oz) chicken	2 sprigs fresh parsley
1 onion, peeled and chopped	5 fresh bay leaves
2 tbsp olive oil	salt and pepper
2 leeks, white part only, sliced	50g (1³/₄oz) butter
2 carrots, peeled and sliced	2 tbsp plain flour
2 celery stalks, sliced	3 egg yolks
100ml (3¹/₂fl oz) dry white wine	125ml (4fl oz) single cream
300ml (10fl oz) chicken stock	2 tbsp chopped fresh thyme leaves
10 whole cloves	100g (3¹/₂oz) green olives, stoned and sliced

Preheat the oven to 160°C/325°F/gas mark 3.

Cut the chicken into quarters. In a heavy casserole dish, brown the onion in the olive oil, then add the leeks, carrots and celery, and sauté for 5 minutes. Arrange the chicken pieces over the vegetables, then pour in the wine and stock. Add the cloves, parsley and bay leaves, and season.

Place the casserole in the oven and cook for about 1¹/₂ hours, or until the chicken is cooked. When ready, take out of the oven and keep warm. Pour out the cooking liquid and reserve.

In a shallow pan, melt the butter, add the flour and cook until light brown. Gradually add most of the cooking liquid, stirring until the sauce is thick and smooth. Mix the egg yolks and cream and add to the fricasee sauce. Do not let this boil, just simmer gently.

Add the thyme and green olives to the sauce, and pour into the casserole with the chicken. Simmer for just 2-3 minutes, then serve with plain boiled white rice.

White Borscht

Serves 6

This recipe was given to me by my Polish friend Robert, a chef in Wodka, one of London's best Polish restaurants. I have had many different *zureks* (*gzureks*), but this is the best – and certainly the richest – by far. It is basically a sour soup flavoured with a *kwas*, meaning literally 'acid', a name that indicates a special fermented sauce used to sour soups. White borscht stock or sour rye stock is sold in every Eastern European deli and is a key ingredient in this recipe. It is sold in bottles and its main components are water, sour rye flour and garlic. If you are unable to obtain it, then add about 3 tbsp white wine-vinegar instead. White sausage is available in delis as well as some large supermarkets.

3 tbsp vegetable oil
2 large onions, peeled and finely sliced
100g (3¹/₂oz) pancetta, thinly sliced
2 carrots, peeled and grated
3 large potatoes, peeled and cubed
4 tbsp dried marjoram

4 bay leaves
3 tbsp horseradish cream
150ml (5fl oz) sour rye stock (*see* above)
1.5 litres (2³/₄ pints) chicken stock
200g (7oz) Polish white sausage, thinly sliced
6 hard-boiled eggs, shelled and chopped

Heat the oil in a large saucepan. Add the onions and sauté over a medium heat until soft and transparent, about 5 minutes.

Add the *pancetta*, carrots and potatoes, and cook for a further 5 minutes. Add the marjoram, bay leaves, horseradish, sour rye stock and chicken stock. Bring to the boil and simmer for 10 minutes.

Add the white sausage and simmer for a further 15 minutes.

Serve hot with chopped hard-boiled egg on top.

Moldavian Aubergine Moussaka

Serves 6

This moussaka from Moldavia is finished with a wonderful rich topping made from feta and yoghurt or sour cream. When fried, aubergine absorbs massive amounts of oil, so you must work quickly; at the same time you must make sure that the aubergine is fully cooked or it will taste bitter.

3 large aubergines, 800g (1lb 12oz) in weight
vegetable oil
salt and pepper
1 large onion, peeled and finely chopped
400g (14oz) lamb mince
1 x 400g can plum tomatoes
$1/2$ tsp marigold or saffron

$1/2$ tsp ground cumin
1 bunch fresh parsley, finely chopped
2 large beef tomatoes
250g (9oz) feta cheese, crumbled
200ml (7fl oz) thick plain yoghurt
2 large eggs, beaten

Peel the aubergines and slice them lengthwise into 5mm thick slices.

In a large and heavy non-stick pan, heat some oil and sauté the aubergine slices, a few at a time, turning them over and making sure that they are evenly browned and cooked. Using a slotted spoon, transfer to kitchen paper to drain off the excess fat. Sprinkle with salt. Repeat this until you have cooked all the aubergine slices, adding more oil when needed. Keep the aubergine slices in a cool place until ready to use.

Preheat the oven to 180°C/350°F/gas mark 4, and have ready a medium 15 x 10 x 4cm (6 x 4 x 2 inch) baking dish, lightly greased with oil.

Now prepare the moussaka filling. In a large, heavy saucepan, warm 2 tbsp oil and sauté the onion for about 5 minutes. Add the lamb mince and cook until the meat is browned. Add the canned tomatoes and their juices, the marigold and cumin, and simmer for a further 10 minutes. Season to taste and add the parsley.

Slice the large beef tomatoes horizontally into 5mm slices and keep aside until ready to use.

To assemble the moussaka, line the bottom of the dish with a third of the aubergine slices, slightly overlapping, and top with half of the lamb mixture, then cover again with half of the remaining aubergine slices and the second half of the meat mixture. Cover with the remaining aubergine slices and finish with the tomato slices.

Cover the dish tightly with foil and place in a large oven tray half filled with hot water. Bake for 45 minutes.

Meanwhile, in a bowl mix the feta, yoghurt and eggs. Remove the foil from the dish and the baking dish from the water bath. Pour the topping over the moussaka, and return it to the oven for another 15 minutes to brown. Serve hot.

Zurek

Cumin and Cardamom-Scented Spring Lamb Fillet

Serves 4

This dish has flavours that are reminiscent of Georgia, Turkey and Armenia. Exotic and oriental spices, such as cumin, cardamom and coriander, are not exclusive to Middle Eastern cuisine. Bulgarian cooking relies heavily on cumin, paprika and cinnamon, something that is inherited from years under Ottoman rule.

400g (14oz) boned neck of lamb
1/2 tsp ground cinnamon
1/4 tsp black peppercorns, crushed
1/2 tsp ground cumin
1/2 tsp ground cardamom

1/4 tsp ground coriander
1/4 tsp salt
5 tbsp olive oil
a handful of fresh mint leaves

Preheat the oven to 180°C/350°F/gas mark 4.

To prepare the lamb, combine the cinnamon, pepper, cumin, cardamom, coriander and salt in a bowl. Season the lamb with the spice rub and place it, covered, in the refrigerator for 4 hours.

To cook the lamb, sauté it in the olive oil over a medium heat for about 5 minutes on each side. To finish the cooking, place it in the oven for 12 minutes, or slightly longer if you like it well-done. Reserve any cooking juices. Keep the lamb in a warm place until ready to serve.

To serve, cut the lamb into 16 slices, season to taste and arrange on a plate. Decorate with mint.

Bigos
Hunter's Stew

Serves 4-6

Bigos is Poland's national dish. There are a lot of recipes advising how to cook hunter's stew, and each family in Poland has its own version with a secret ingredient or twist. One thing is for sure, though: it always contains the catch of the day – whatever the hunter brings home after a day of hunting – smoked meat and lots of sauerkraut!

I remember sauerkraut in communist Bulgaria, when there was little food in the shops, especially during the long, cold winters. My mother would prepare plenty of sauerkraut in a big barrel while cabbage was plentiful during the spring and summer, so it would be ready to use in the winter months. Oh, the taste of homemade sauerkraut – the crunchy, sour delight stored on every balcony of every apartment, not only in my native Bulgaria, but in Russia, the Baltic countries, Ukraine and Poland too.

Luckily, over here sauerkraut is sold almost everywhere in jars, so there is no need to make your own. *Bigos* is best made a few days in advance and cooked slowly for at least an hour 2 days after the initial day of cooking, so that the flavours are allowed to develop fully.

2 onions, peeled and finely chopped	600g (1lb 5oz) tomatoes, skinned/chopped
35g (1^1/$_4$oz) butter	400ml (14fl oz) strong chicken stock
^{1}/$_2$ tsp caraway seeds	250g (9oz) lean pork belly
^{1}/$_2$ tsp juniper berries, crushed	1 large apple, peeled and grated
1.25kg (2lb 12oz) sauerkraut	250g (9oz) *cabanos* sausage, sliced

Fry the onions in the butter in a heavy saucepan over a medium heat until just lightly brown. Add the juniper berries and caraway seeds.

Squeeze the excess juices from the sauerkraut, and add it to the onion, stirring well. Add the tomatoes and cook for 2-3 minutes, than add the chicken stock and pork. Cook with the lid on for about 30 minutes, then add the apple and sausage. Simmer the stew, covered, on a low heat for 1-1^1/$_2$ hours. Cool, cover and refrigerate.

Cook for an hour on a low heat the next day and for a final hour on the day of serving. Ensure the meat is cooked through. *Bigos* freezes well, so I usually do a lot of it and store it in the freezer in smaller containers. A delicious *bigos* is all about slow cooking!

Veal Goulash Pies

Serves 6

The British love a good pie, so I thought I would include this recipe, which was kindly given to me by Magdi Bartoc, who prepared it for me during one of my visits to Hungary. It looks great and is an alternative way of preparing goulash. Magdi made her own pastry but I have found that shop-bought shortcrust pasty works very well.

400g (14oz) shortcrust pastry
1 egg yolk, whisked
sour cream, to serve

Goulash Filling
800g (1lb 12oz) veal shoulder, cut
   into 3cm (1^{1}/4 inch) cubes
1 tbsp cornflour
salt and pepper

4 tbsp olive oil
1 onion, peeled and thinly sliced
2 garlic cloves, peeled and crushed
^{1}/2 tsp caraway seeds
2 tsp sweet (noble) paprika
100ml (3^{1}/2fl oz) chicken stock
1 x 400g can chopped tomatoes
2 tbsp chopped fresh marjoram leaves, or
   1 tbsp dried

Preheat the oven to 200ºC/400ºF/gas mark 6. Place the veal and cornflour in a large mixing bowl and mix well to coat the veal pieces. Season with salt and pepper.

Heat half of the oil in a heavy sauté pan and sauté the coated veal, a few cubes at a time so they can be browned evenly without crowding. When all the meat has browned, remove to one side.

Add the remaining oil to the pan with the onion, garlic and caraway seeds, stirring all the time. Remove from the heat and add the paprika, stirring well and returning again to the stove to continue cooking (if you add paprika on the heat it will burn and become bitter). Add the veal, stock and tomatoes and simmer, uncovered, for about 50 minutes, until the cooking juices have reduced by half. Add the marjoram and let it cool completely.

Roll two-thirds of the pastry to 4mm thick and cut out 6 large circles about 12-15cm (5-6 inch) in diameter. Line 6 mini tart tins, about 10cm (4 inches) in diameter, with the pastry circles. Line each pastry case with greaseproof paper and fill them with dried beans or baking weights. Blind-bake for 15 minutes, then remove the paper and beans and bake for 10 more minutes. Remove the tart shells from the oven, and reduce the oven temperature to 180ºC/350ºF/gas mark 4.

Roll the remaining pastry to 4mm thick and cut out 6 circles that are large enough to cover the tops of the individual tarts.

Spoon the goulash into all 6 pastry cases and place the pastry rounds over each of the dishes, pressing the sides on to each other to seal well. Cut a cross on the top of each pie and brush with egg yolk. Bake for 30 minutes, until golden. Serve with sour cream.

Gulyas
Goulash Soup
Serves 6-8

The Hungarian dish. There are so many "authentic" recipes for goulash; it is difficult to find the real one. The origins of goulash go back to the Middle Ages, when shepherds would cut their meat into pieces, cook it with onions slowly so all the liquid would evaporate, then dry the meat in the sun, putting the dried meat into a bag made from a sheep's stomach. When on their travels and wanting a meal, they would add water to the dried pieces of meat and reheat it. Depending on how much water they added, the meal would become goulash soup or stew. In Hungary, goulash soup is found on every street corner, and it is different to what we would normally think of as goulash.

3 tbsp vegetable oil

1 large onion, peeled and chopped

800g (1lb 12oz) good stewing beef, cut into 3cm (1^1/$_4$ inch) cubes

1 garlic clove, peeled and crushed

^{1}/$_2$ tsp caraway seeds

2 tbsp sweet (noble) paprika

1.5 litres (2^3/$_4$ pints) water

2 medium tomatoes, chopped

1 sweet green pepper, seeded and thinly sliced

300g (10^1/$_2$oz) potatoes, peeled and cubed

salt and pepper

Heat the oil over a medium heat in a heavy casserole-type saucepan. Add the onion and sauté, but do not brown. When the onion turns transparent, add the beef and stir to sauté the meat with the onions. Add the garlic and caraway seeds.

Remove the pan from the heat and add the paprika, stirring constantly to make sure it is absorbed well by the meat. The pan must be removed from the heat to add the paprika because paprika has a high sugar content; if added directly over heat it would burn and become bitter. Paprika is never added on direct heat.

Add the water and simmer gently for at least an hour. Check that the meat is cooked by testing a small piece. If you are happy with it, add the tomatoes, pepper and potatoes. Season and simmer for 30 minutes. Serve hot with *galuska (see* page 128), the dumplings that are traditionally served with goulash.

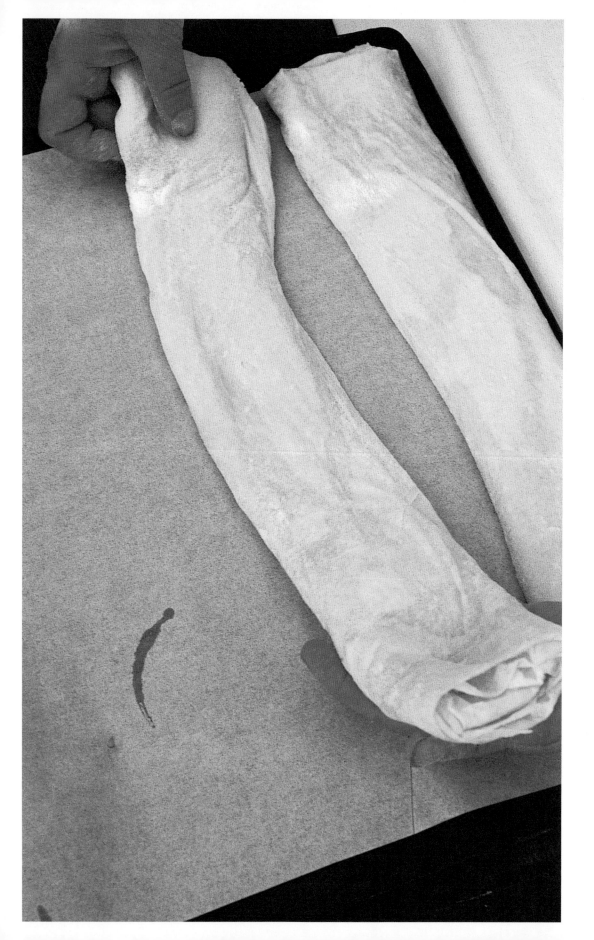

Hungarian Poppy Seed and Apple Strudel

Serves 6

Retes, pronounced "retesh", is the star of Hungarian patisserie, the finest and most delicate of flaky pastry, wrapped around various sweet or savoury fillings. To make the pastry from scratch is truly an art, involving huge amounts of time and patience. I am more than satisfied with using ready-made strudel pastry or filo pastry, which provides excellent results. It is widely available in British supermarkets.

50g (1³/₄oz) butter, melted

12 large sheets fresh filo pastry, plus
   2 extra in case you need more

5 tbsp ground almonds

2 tsp poppy seeds

2 tsp icing sugar

Poppy Seed and Apple Filling

75-100ml water (2¹/₂-3¹/₂fl oz)

4 tbsp caster sugar

4 tbsp golden sultanas

2 tbsp poppy seeds, ground

3 apples, peeled and thinly sliced

Preheat the oven to 180°C/350°F/gas mark 4.

Make the filling first. Place the water and sugar in a small saucepan, bring to the boil, and then simmer for no longer than 2 minutes to dissolve the sugar. Add the sultanas and ground poppy seeds and let it all cool.

In a large mixing bowl, place the apples and add the cooled sugar syrup, mixing well.

Prepare a large baking sheet by brushing it with some butter. Start laying filo sheets on top of it, one at a time, brushing liberally with butter in between and sprinkling generously with the ground almonds. Once you have used 3 filo sheets, spread a thin layer of apple and poppy seed filling and continue with the filo sheets, repeating the same again after the next 3, and again after 3, until all 12 filo pastry sheets have been used. Roll up like a Swiss roll and tuck in the ends. Turn the strudel seam-side down and brush with the remaining butter.

Sprinkle with the whole poppy seeds and bake for 25-30 minutes, until golden brown. Cool completely before you cut, dust with icing sugar and serve.

Makowiec
Polish Poppy Seed and Almond Cake

Serves 8

Using poppy seeds in desserts is a great tradition in the cuisines of Russia, Ukraine, Hungary and Poland. They can be ground into a powder and used in various desserts. This cake is called *makowiec* in Poland and is popular in café shops.

325ml (11fl oz) milk	***Poppy Seed and Almond Filling***
60g (2^1/$_4$oz) butter	250g (9oz) poppy seeds
85g (3oz) caster sugar	100g (3^1/$_2$oz) caster sugar
15g (^{1}/$_2$oz) fresh yeast	60g (2^1/$_4$oz) butter, cubed
1 egg	150g (5^1/$_2$oz) ground almonds
650g (1lb 7oz) plain flour	zest of 3 lemons
1 egg white, lightly beaten	4 tsp clear honey

Bring 275ml of the milk to the boil in a medium, heavy based saucepan, then add the butter and 65g sugar, stirring. Remove from the heat and leave to cool.

Place the remaining milk in a small pan and warm on a low heat until just lukewarm. Place in a bowl and add the yeast, egg, remaining sugar and 1 tbsp flour, and mix well. Keep in a warm place until foamy.

Transfer the milk and butter mixture to a large bowl and add the yeast mixture. Stir to combine and slowly add the remaining flour. Mix well, then knead the dough on a lightly floured surface in front of you until smooth and elastic. Stand the dough in a bowl for an hour, until doubled in volume.

Meanwhile, make the poppy seed filling. Place the poppy seeds in a large pan and cover with water. Simmer for 40 minutes and drain. Put the poppy seeds through a grinder and grind to powder. Place in a bowl and add all the remaining ingredients.

Preheat the oven to 180°C/350°F/gas mark 4.

When the dough is ready to cook, divide into 2 and roll each piece into a rectangle, 20 x 40cm (8 x 16 inch). Spread half of the filling over each rectangle and roll up to form 2 Swiss rolls. Brush with egg white and bake for 25 minutes. Cool on a cooling rack.

the glory of my valley
THE FRUITS OF AUTUMN

And our distant, coldish summer season,

Like playful winter flashes by

Until we barely make out.... It's gone.

The fact we solemnly deny.

The savour of autumn's in the air.

Eugene Onegin (a novel in verse), *Complete Collected Works in 6 Tomes,* Alexander Pushkin [6]

Autumn brings golden harvests in the Northern hemisphere: the days are starting to shorten, the light is kinder. Gone are the red berries, juicy cherries and pink-fleshed peaches, but instead the markets are loaded with perfumed quinces, mellow figs, golden clusters of luscious grapes, crimson pomegranates and succulent plums of endless variety.

This was the time of year when my mother would get the whole house mobilized and organized military style. We would buy the fresh produce of late summer and early autumn and prepare delicious fig and plum jams, preserved lemons, tomatoes, pepper relish, fruit compotes and syrups. We'd pour these into a rich array of old-fashioned jars of all shapes and sizes.

There are various ways in which foods are preserved in Eastern Europe, with drying and pickling being the main methods. In Hungary, where they have a wonderful plum harvest, plums are pitted and stuffed with pieces of walnut before being left to dry. The specialties of our house were the sauerkraut and pickled gherkins. My mum would set the cucumbers in a jar lined with perfumed walnut and raspberry leaves; she would add dill seeds and fresh dill, some mustard seeds and a small piece of freshly sliced fennel before finally topping up with a homemade vinegar marinade that produced an exquisite sweet-and-sour taste.

Aubergine Stacks with Pumpkin and Feta Cheese

Serves 4

Aubergine and pumpkin are two of my favourite ingredients, and putting them together works beautifully. My father's version includes crumbled feta cheese scattered among the layers of crispy aubergine. There must be more than 100 aubergine recipes in my native Bulgarian cuisine, inherited mainly, I imagine, from when Bulgaria was under Turkish rule.

2 small aubergines
salt and pepper
1 tbsp plain flour
20ml (^{3}/4fl oz) olive oil

10g (^{1}/2oz) butter
600g (1lb 5oz) pumpkin flesh, roasted and and chopped
2 tbsp finely chopped fresh oregano leaves
150g (5^1/2oz) sheep's feta cheese, chopped

Preheat the oven to 200°C/400°F/gas mark 6.

Trim, wash and dry the aubergines. Cut into 5mm slices lengthwise. Season with salt and pepper, and coat with flour.

Heat the oil in a non-stick shallow frying pan, and gently fry each aubergine slice on both sides until lightly browned. Drain on kitchen paper.

Melt the butter in the wiped frying pan, and add the cooked pumpkin, the oregano and feta cheese. Stir and cook for a few minutes.

Starting with the largest of the aubergine slices, assemble on a baking sheet 4 piles of aubergine, interlayered the slices with the pumpkin-cheese mixture and finishing each pile with the smallest of the aubergine slices.

Bake for 5 minutes and serve hot.

Bulgur Salad with Grapes and Pistachios

Serves 4

Barley is my favourite grain; indeed, I was brought up on a diet of barley and rice. My mum used to make this delicious, crunchy salad to accompany her juicy *kufteta* (meatballs). We had vines in our summer-house, and from its grapes my father would produce what he claimed was the most superior wine in the vicinity. But then again winemaking was almost most people's pastime and he wasn't the only person to make this claim. Our grapes were like giant sapphires, full of sweetness and summer zest.

250g (9oz) bulgur wheat
2 large ripe tomatoes, finely diced
$^1/_2$ green pepper, deseeded and chopped
$^1/_2$ cucumber, peeled and finely sliced
85g (3oz) white seedless grapes, halved
1 small garlic clove, peeled and crushed

salt and pepper
40ml (1$^1/_2$fl oz) olive oil
juice of 1$^1/_2$ lemon
5 tbsp chopped fresh parsley
3 tbsp chopped fresh mint
3 tbsp shelled pistachios, lightly toasted

Cook the bulgur wheat in plenty of hot water until soft, about 15 minutes. Drain well and keep to one side.

In a large bowl, mix together the tomatoes, green pepper, cucumber, grapes and garlic. Add the bulgur wheat and mix well. Season with salt and pepper, then add the olive oil and lemon juice, and finally mix in the parsley and mint.

Let the salad stand in the fridge for about 2 hours. Sprinkle with toasted pistachios to serve.

Roast Pheasant Stuffed with Barley and Golden Sultanas

Serves 4

This is a version of a Georgian recipe I had at the home of my friend Tamara. Her husband would go hunting in season and she had a wealth of recipes for all sorts of gamy delicacies.

2 cock pheasants, ready to cook
85g (3oz) butter
salt and pepper

Stuffing
200g (7oz) pearl barley
2 tbsp olive oil
1 shallot, peeled and finely chopped
100g (3¹/₂oz) golden sultanas
2 tbsp chopped fresh parsley
juice and finely grated zest of ¹/₂ lemon

For the stuffing, cook the barley in some hot water for about 20 minutes, until soft. Drain and set aside. Heat the oil in a heavy frying pan, and cook and stir the shallot, sultanas and cooked barley for a few minutes. Add the parsley and lemon zest and juice. Cool. When cold, stuff into the cavity of the pheasants; don't worry if the stuffing spills out

Meanwhile, preheat the oven to 180°C/350°F/gas mark 4.

Smear the birds with butter, sprinkle with salt and pepper to taste, and roast for about an hour, basting at regular intervals, until cooked through. Carve and serve with the stuffing.

Veal, Almond and Sour-Cherry Stuffed Vine Leaves

Makes 40

These stuffed vine leaves were Auntie Ester's *dolmeh*. The sweet, fruity flavours are evidence of Jewish influence; while adding some sour cherries or plums supplements the acidity of the dish. Use fresh vine leaves when you can. Vine leaves stuffed with various fillings are common in Eastern Europe, and can be found in Bulgaria, Romania, Albania and Bosnia, among others. They are little cylinder-like rolls of tender leaves, and can also be prepared as a vegetarian dish. The vegetarian version is a typical Christmas Eve dish in Bulgaria. As much as I would love to proclaim the dish to be Bulgarian, I have to admit that it was the Turkish who invented it.

50 fresh vine leaves or 1 x 300g packet
  vine leaves in brine
2 tbsp olive oil
1 medium shallot, peeled and finely chopped
400g (14oz) lean veal, finely minced
150g ($5^1/_2$oz) long-grain rice
about 100ml ($3^1/_2$fl oz) water or stock

$^1/_2$ tsp ground cumin
salt and pepper
85g (3oz) flaked almonds
85g (3oz) dried sour cherries
a small bunch of fresh parsley, finely chopped
2 tbsp chopped fresh mint

If you can find fresh vine leaves, simply poach them in hot water for a minute before using. Otherwise use cured leaves from a packet or jar – they're sold widely in British supermarkets; simply remove them and drain, place them in a colander and pour hot water over them before draining.

In a heavy, deep frying pan, heat the olive oil and cook the shallot over a medium heat until soft. Add the veal mince and cook until the meat is browned, stirring all the time. Add the rice and continue to stir. The mixture will need a little liquid now, so add most of the water or stock, and simmer for about 10 minutes, adding the cumin and some salt and pepper.

When the liquid has mostly been absorbed, add the almonds and sour cherries, and switch off the heat. Cover the pan with a clean tea towel and then the lid, and leave to stand for 10 minutes. Add the parsley and mint and mix.

Line a large, heavy, casserole dish with about 5 vine leaves (I usually use the broken leaves that I am unable to stuff, there are always some…). Lay a vine leaf on a work surface, stalk towards you, and put a heaped tsp of the veal mixture just above the point where the stalk is, just below the middle of the leaf. Fold the stalk side up, wrapping the mixture almost immediately, and then fold both sides of the leaf into the centre and roll the leaf up so you have a cylinder. Place each stuffed leaf in the lined pan, join-side down. Do this with all the leaves and stuffing, packing them tightly.

Add water to come three-quarters up the height of the stuffed vine leaves. Cover with about 3-5 leaves and place a plate just slightly smaller than the pan you are cooking in on top to weigh the stuffed leaves down. Cook over a slow and gentle heat on top of the stove for about 45 minutes. Leave them to cool in their cooking juices. Serve with Greek yoghurt.

Braised Lamb Shanks with Barley and Egg and Lemon Sauce

Serves 4

The usual way of preparing lamb shanks is to braise them in a rich red wine or tomato sauce, but this recipe is lighter than that. It comes from the region around the Caucasus mountains, and the original version is cooked with saffron or marigold. Egg and lemon sauce is often prepared in the kitchens of Bulgaria, Hungary, Azerbaijan and Georgia.

2 tbsp olive oil
4 large lamb shanks
4 small shallots, peeled and finely chopped
4 garlic cloves, peeled and minced
zest of 2 lemons
a small bunch of fresh parsley, finely chopped
5 bay leaves
1 litre (1³/4 pints) lamb stock or water, and more if needed
salt and pepper
250g (9oz) pearl barley, rinsed and drained

Egg and Lemon Sauce
200ml (7fl oz) cooking liquid
1 tsp cornflour
juice of 1 lemon
2 large egg yolks
a small bunch of fresh coriander, finely chopped

Heat the olive oil in a heavy, deep casserole dish. Brown the shanks well, about 10 minutes. Remove and keep warm.

Add the shallots to the oil in the dish and cook until soft, about 12 minutes. Return the lamb to the dish. Add the garlic, lemon zest, some chopped parsley, the bay leaves and stock. Season to taste. Bring to the boil and then simmer, covered, for about an hour.

Preheat the oven to 170°C/325°F/gas mark 3.

Now add the barley and about 100ml water to the casserole, and bring to the boil. Place the casserole, still covered, in the oven, and cook until the barley is done and the lamb is tender, about an hour. Once cooked, strain and measure 200ml of the cooking juice and put to one side. Sprinkle the dish generously with the remaining parsley.

To make the sauce, bring the reserved liquid to a simmer in a small saucepan. Mix some water with the cornflour to a smooth paste, then add the lemon juice and egg yolks. Add this to the simmering liquid and stir well for a few minutes, until cooked and thickened. Season to taste and stir in the finely chopped coriander.

Serve the lamb shanks on top of a small pile of barley and spoon over the sauce.

Rabbit with Plums and White Wine

Serves 4

I am very fond of rabbit, but I realize that many people may feel uncomfortable about eating it. Rabbit is delicious and almost fat-free. It is usually a soft, tender, chicken-like meat, but it must never be overcooked or it will get rather tough.

3 tbsp olive oil
1 large rabbit, cut into pieces
salt and pepper
1 onion, peeled and thinly sliced
3 garlic cloves, peeled and crushed

100g (3^1/$_2$oz) pancetta cubes
300g (10^1/$_2$oz) ripe plums, stoned and halved
300ml (10fl oz) white wine
200ml (7fl oz) chicken stock
a handful of fresh sage leaves, chopped

Preheat the oven to 180°C/350°F/gas mark 4.

In a large non-stick casserole dish, heat the oil and add the rabbit pieces, turning frequently to brown evenly. Season with salt and pepper.

Add the onion, garlic and pancetta and continue cooking for another 5 minutes. Keep stirring all the time.

Add the plums, white wine and stock and mix well. Cover the casserole and cook in the oven for an hour, until the rabbit is tender. The plums will be mushy and will give the stew a lovely texture.

Serve hot, sprinkled with fresh sage and accompanied by some crusty bread.

Peach and Sour Cream Napoleons

Serves 4

This is what I call "deconstructed strudel". If you have not worked with filo pastry before, you will be amazed by how easy it is. This is a quick and delicate dessert. You can also use plums and apricots instead of peaches.

4 large sheets filo pastry
4 tsp melted butter
6 tsp ground almonds
200ml (7fl oz) sour cream

3 tbsp mascarpone cheese
4 tsp caster sugar
2 fresh ripe peaches, cut into thin strips
icing sugar

Preheat the oven to 180°C/350°F/gas mark 4.

Arrange 1 filo sheet on a large baking tray that has been lined with parchment paper, and brush generously with some melted butter. Sprinkle with a quarter of the ground almonds. Top with the other 3 layers of filo, butter and almonds. Cut into 12 rectangles and bake until golden brown and crisp, about 10 minutes. Cool on a rack.

In a small bowl, mix together the sour cream, mascarpone and 2 tsp caster sugar.

Place 1 filo rectangle on a serving plate and place some sour cream mixture on top, followed by some thin slices of ripe peach. Add another layer of filo and again top with the sour cream mixture and fresh peach slices, finally finishing with a filo layer. Make 3 more Napoleons in the same way.

Dust with icing sugar and serve immediately.

Poached Plums with Rose-water Sorbet

Serves 4

Rose-water can be found in all regions of Bulgaria. The country's "valley of the roses" provides the highest-quality rose oils and extracts in the world (the most well-known perfume houses buy their rose oils from this valley). Rose-water is a distillation of red rose petals, and has the intense perfumed flavour of its source. It creates the scent of an old-fashioned rose garden in full bloom, but at the same time it has a surprising spicy and smoky quality. To make sugar syrup, just use any basic recipe from a good desserts cookbook; it is simply a mixture of sugar and water.

200g (7oz) plums, halved and stoned
150ml (5fl oz) sugar syrup
4 cloves
juice of 1^1/$_2$ lemons
6 tbsp rose-water

Sorbet
350ml (12fl oz) sugar syrup
375ml (14fl oz) water
4 tbsp rose-water
juice of 1 lemon
1 egg white, lightly beaten

Place the plums in the sugar syrup and add the cloves and lemon juice. Simmer on a medium heat, covered, for about 10 minutes or until the plums are soft. Stir in the rose-water.

To make the sorbet, combine the sugar syrup, water, rose-water and lemon juice and pour into an ice-cream machine. Churn for about 5 minutes, or until it becomes opaque. Add the egg white, while still churning. Continue until the sorbet is firm enough to serve, or store in a container and place in the freezer.

To serve, place some warm poached plums on each plate with scoops of the rose-water sorbet. Spoon over some syrup.

Baked Quinces in Quince and Cinnamon Syrup

Serves 6

Aphrodite, the Greek goddess of love, was known to consider apples sacred. But historians believe the apples favoured by Aphrodite were really quinces. Indeed, the legendary golden apple of Hesperides that Paris gave to Aphrodite was really a quince. The quince posseses the finest perfume that a fruit can have: subtle, delicate and long-lasting. When quinces are cooked with sugar, they change colour and texture. They transform from pale yellow and woody-fleshed into brownish-red in colour and rich in flavour.

6 quinces
juice of 2 lemons
200g (7oz) caster sugar
1 vanilla pod, split lengthways
300ml (10fl oz) water

5 cloves
1 small cinnamon stick

To Serve
200ml (7fl oz) sour cream

Peel 4 of the quinces and cut them into quarters. Remove and discard the cores and place the quince flesh in a large, heavy ovenproof baking dish with a lid, arranged in a single layer. Pour over the lemon juice to prevent discoloration.

Meanwhile, use the remaining 2 quinces to make the quince syrup. Peel, core and chop them coarsely. Place them in a large pan with 100g of the sugar, the scraped-out vanilla seeds and the pod. Add enough water to cover. Bring to the boil and simmer for about an hour, or until the quinces are very soft and dark red, and the liquid has turned syrupy. Strain the syrup and discard the quince pulp and vanilla pod.

Meanwhile, preheat the oven to 160°C/325°F/gas mark 3.

Pour the syrup over the quince quarters that you prepared earlier, adding the cloves, cinnamon and remaining sugar. Make sure the quinces are covered by the syrup and place a piece of baking paper over to keep the fruit submerged. Cover the baking dish with foil and cook for an hour or more, until the quinces are soft to the touch and red in colour.

To serve, place 4 quince quarters with some syrup on each dessert plate and add a good dollop of sour cream.

Prune and Walnut Cheesecake

Serves 8-10

The Polish love their cheesecakes and have many in their dessert repertoire. Try to get hold of Polish cream cheese when preparing this one; if you can't, then a standard cream cheese will do fine. This cheesecake is baked, and I have used brioche for the base. I also recommend you use a square or round baking tin with removable sides. The Eastern European Jewish émigrés adopted the cheesecake as a Jewish cake, and initially prepared it to celebrate *Shavuot* (the festival marking the conclusion of the seven weeks following *Pesach*, or Passover).

350g (12oz) prunes, stoned
juice and zest of 4 lemons
1 cinnamon stick
2 fresh bay leaves
100g (3^1/$_2$oz) butter, melted, plus extra
   for buttering
1 x 250g (9oz) brioche loaf

100g (3^1/$_2$oz) shelled walnuts
a pinch of freshly grated nutmeg
250g (9oz) Polish cream cheese
200g (7oz) caster sugar
400g (14oz) mascarpone cheese
4 large eggs

Place the prunes, half the lemon zest and juice, the cinnamon stick and bay leaves in a medium saucepan and bring to the boil, then almost immediately turn down the heat to simmer for 3-4 minutes. Cool and let this stand overnight.

Preheat the oven to 160°C/325°F/gas mark 3.

Butter the base and sides of a 24cm (10 inch) square or round baking tin. Cut the brioche into cubes and place in a food processor with the walnuts, then process until finely chopped. Put the brioche and walnut mixture in a large bowl with the nutmeg, melted butter and 50g sugar. Mix well and press the mixture gently over the base of the buttered baking tin. Refrigerate until firm.

To make the filling, beat the cheeses together with the remaining lemon zest and juice, the remaining sugar, and the eggs. Add the latter one by one, beating well in between to combine well.

Drain the prunes and cut them into small pieces. Place them all over the cheesecake base, then pour over the filling, smoothing the top.

Bake for about an hour, or until the filling has set. Cool completely before serving.

Meringue Rice Puddings

Serves 6

My boys love these, and when I was a girl growing up in Bulgaria I was no different. I would forever pester my mother to make rice pudding; to go a week without one would have been scandalous! The sweet aroma of scented, delicate rice pudding would waft around our apartment on Sundays, a truly comforting, cosy Sunday smell. A Jewish friend of my father's, Avram Avramov, told me that white-rice dishes, in Jewish cooking, symbolized the purity of the Torah and were offered at a particular celebration referred to as "The Feast of the Roses", sometimes sprinkled with rose petals during prayers. This pudding is scented with rose-water and sprinkled with red rose petals.

200g (7oz) pudding rice
400ml (14fl oz) double cream
700ml (1¼ pints) full-fat milk
150g (5½oz) caster sugar

5 tbsp rose-water
3 egg whites
pink rose petals

Preheat the oven to 180°C/350°F/gas mark 4.

Put the rice and 270ml double cream in a heavy saucepan, place over a medium heat and cook for 2-3 minutes. Mix well and then add the milk and 120g caster sugar. Cook on a low heat for another 10-15 minutes, until the rice grains are soft. When the liquid has more or less evaporated, add the remaining double cream and the rose-water.

Whip the egg whites, then whisk in the remaining sugar.

Pour the rice pudding into 6 individual soufflé-type dishes and pipe the meringue mix on top of each pudding using a piping bag, or just spoon it over.

Place in the oven for 8-10 minutes, until the tops of the meringues have become slightly golden in colour. When cooler, but still warm, serve sprinkled with a few rose petals.

DUMPLING MAGIC

All that Patsuk had to do is just think about it, open his mouth, stare at the vareniki *and open his mouth even wider. At that very time, a* varenik *jumped out of the platter, splashed into the* smetana, *then flipped over and at once leapt into his mouth. Patsuk ate it, then once more he opened his mouth, and just like before another* varenik *put on the same show. All that was left for Patsuk to do was to munch it up and swallow it.*

The Nights in the Village near Dikanka, Nikolai Gogol,
Complete Collected Works Volume 1[7]

In this Gogol story, the hero Patsuk (a sorceror) brings *vareniki* to life both literally and figuratively. This is just one of many stories in Russian literature that is devoted to food and, in particular, the dumpling. To talk about the cuisines of Eastern Europe without mentioning the myriad dumplings is unthinkable. There are hundreds of dumpling recipes, each of which has endless variations. We all love dumplings: they are cosy and fluffy, comforting and satisfying, homely and even fashionable and familiar, like the Chinese *dim sum,* the Japanese *gyoza* and Indian *samosa.* The Polish *pierogi,* Russian *pirozhki,* and Hungarian *galuska* or Ukrainian *vareniky* and *pampushki* are no less delicious just because they are less known to us in the West. The names sound cosy and affectionate; dumplings' names are usually diminutive and almost impossible to translate.

Dumplings are prepared as a main meal, as an accompaniment or as a snack. They make perfect vodka-chasers and are a typical accompaniment to toasts. They are usually light, despite their reputation of being stodgy (brought about, probably in the British mind at least, by the suet-based balls cooked in a stew). Eastern dumplings come as mouth-watering dough, grain or potato parcels, with savoury or sweet fillings, in many shapes and sizes, and cooked in many ways.

The must-have dumpling for Hungarians is the *galuska,* an egg-and-flour creation cooked in boiling water. The upper classes eat it as an accompaniment to main meals, but the poor have it as a main meal with melted butter. Ukrainians eat *galushky* and *vareniky* on an almost daily basis; the latter is made from a pasta dough and filled with anything from cheese to meat to poppy seeds.

The Polish have a dumpling repertoire of their own. *Pierogi* are small, soft, almost velvety filled dough purses. *Pierogi-tarte* are made from grated potatoes and filled with a mixture of bacon, onion and cream cheese. Both are cooked in boiling water. Russian *pirozhki* are just as delicious, but baked in a hot oven and served crisp, filled with whatever is to hand, depending on the occasion and season. In Bulgaria, veal and parsley dumplings are perfect for soups and casseroles.

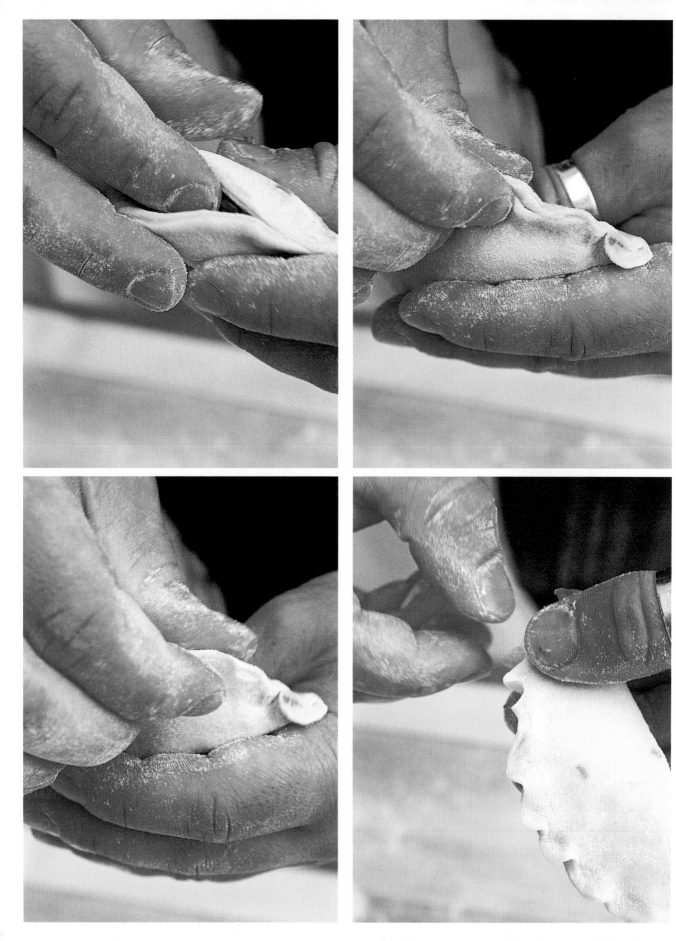

Galuska
Hungarian Dumplings

Serves 6

Galuska are the most famous dumplings in Hungary and are a loyal accompaniment to all *porkolt* dishes (the national paprika stew). *Galuska* are also offered when serving goulash. They can be made from different kinds of dough and are always very, very small. The Ukrainians also have a similar dumpling called *galushki,* made with wheat flour and cut in squares. The names are rather similar, but the tastes and purposes of the two are totally different. The best *galuska* I have ever eaten was at the world-famous Gundel restaurant in Budapest.

2 eggs
1 tsp salt
200ml (7fl oz) water

300g (10^1/$_2$oz) plain flour
a little butter, melted, to serve

Beat the eggs with 1 tsp salt and the water. Add a little flour to make a smooth, thick mixture, then add the rest of the flour and beat with a wooden spoon until the dough is glossy and exceptionally smooth. Adjust with more flour if necessary, until the dough comes away from the sides of the bowl.

Place a large-grade grater on top of a large pan full of salted boiling water and force the dough though the grater directly into the water. Alternatively, roll small dumplings of an even size using your fingers and drop them into the water.

Galuska are done when they rise to the top of the water. Drain them in a colander and serve hot with some melted butter.

Pampushki
Ukrainian Dumplings
Makes 15

Pampushki are a favourite street food in Ukraine. Known also as *ponchiki* in Russia and *ponichki* in Bulgaria, they are sold in the markets and high streets. Their fillings are usually sweet, such as homemade jams and preserves. The most common forms are prepared with a yeast dough, which is allowed to rise, stuffed with conserve, and then fried. This particular recipe is a savoury version of these easy-to-make crispy dumplings, perfect for making at home using potatoes instead of dough.

750g (1lb 10oz) potatoes, peeled
300g (10^1/$_2$oz) cooked mashed potato
vegetable oil for deep-frying

Cheese and Cherry Filling
100g (3^1/$_2$oz) cream cheese
85g (3oz) dried sour cherries
1 tbsp caster sugar
finely grated zest of 2 lemons

Using a large-grade grater, grate the peeled potatoes into a colander and squeeze out as much water as you can. Put in a large bowl, add the mashed potato and mix well.

To make the filling, in a small bowl mix together the cheese, cherries, sugar and lemon zest.

Place a little of the potato mixture in your palm and spread it slightly. Place a tsp of the cheese and cherry mixture on to the potato round and fold over the edges, sealing in the filling entirely. Repeat with the rest of the mixture.

Heat the oil in a large saucepan and, when very hot, drop the *pampushki* in to deep-fry, a couple at a time, for about 8 minutes, until browned and crisp.

Serve hot with a homemade preserve or good-quality jam.

Basil and Caraway Dumplings

Makes 18–20

These are perfect to accompany any sort of hearty winter stew or a traditional goulash. They are delicious and can be cooked in large quantities and frozen to use when needed. I used brioche, which makes the dumplings particularly light, but you can use bread rolls if you prefer.

300g (10^1/$_2$oz) brioche, cut into cubes

100g (3^1/$_2$oz) plain flour

salt and pepper

60g (2^1/$_4$oz) butter

a small bunch of fresh basil, finely chopped

1 tsp caraway seeds

250ml (9fl oz) milk

2 eggs, lightly beaten

200ml (7fl oz) chicken stock

Place the brioche and flour in a large bowl and add 1 tsp salt, stirring well to combine.

Melt the butter in a wide-bottomed pan. Remove from the heat, then add the brioche mixture, basil and caraway seeds, mixing well to combine. Return to the large bowl and add the milk and eggs. Stir with a wooden spoon and let it stand for at least an hour.

Using wet hands, form small rounds of the brioche mixture and place on a lightly floured tray.

Boil the chicken stock and cook the dumplings, a few at a time, for about 12 minutes. Remove and keep warm if you are using immediately, or cool to place in the refrigerator until needed.

Khinkali
Georgian Dumplings

Makes 10–12

No meal in Georgia is complete without *khinkali,* traditional dumplings, which are served in hot or cold weather. They are round, nourishing and satisfying, stuffed with meat or cheese and greens. Shaping them properly is important and comes with experience: the trick is to make as many pleats as possible as you bunch the dough around the stuffing, much like a moneybag. Almost every household in Georgia has some *khinkali* dough at the ready.

300g (10^1/$_2$oz) plain flour
1 tsp salt
175ml (6fl oz) warm water

Cheese Filling
300g (10^1/$_2$oz) sheep's feta cheese
^{1}/$_2$ tsp salt
^{1}/$_4$ tsp freshly ground black pepper
1 large egg, beaten

Mix the flour, salt and warm water to make the dough. It should be neither too firm or too soft; if it's too sticky, add some flour. Knead for 5 minutes and place in a bowl, cover and let it sit for an hour.

Divide the dough into 12 pieces and roll each one into a 10cm (4 inch) round on a floured surface.

To make the filling, crumble the feta cheese into a large bowl using a fork. Add the salt, pepper and egg, and mix well.

Place a large tbsp of the filling on the middle of each pastry round. Folding the edges of the dough in toward the centre, make skirt pleats all the way around the filling. Work clockwise and have each new pleat of dough overlapping the previous pleat, until the filling is securely enclosed.

Finally, twist the pleats together in the centre to seal into a knot. Repeat with all the pastry rounds. Cook the *khinkali* in boiling water for 12 minutes. Serve hot.

Gratin of Cabbage Dumplings

Serves 4–6

This is an old family recipe, passed down through many generations. The dumplings are juicy and light. It makes a perfect side dish for a main meal.

2 tbsp vegetable oil

500g (1lb 2oz) Savoy cabbage, grated

1 tbsp clear honey

250g (9oz) plain flour, plus extra for dusting

25g ($^3/_4$oz) butter

1 egg, lightly beaten

salt and pepper

85g (3oz) mild Cheddar, grated

Preheat the oven to 180°C/350°F/gas mark 4.

Heat the oil in a heavy based pan, add the cabbage, and sweat for a few minutes, until soft. Add the honey and continue to cook, stirring, until the cabbage is slightly brown. Leave to cool.

Meanwhile, place the flour in a bowl, add the butter, egg and a pinch of salt, and mix to a soft dough. Add 1-2 tbsp water to get the right consistency. The dough should be soft and elastic. Roll it out to about 1cm ($^1/_2$ inch) thick on a floured work surface.

Now spread the cool cabbage on to the dough, season with salt and pepper, and roll the dough around the cabbage as you would a Swiss roll. Cut the roll into 3-5cm (1-2 inch) pieces and roll each of these into balls. Have a large saucepan with boiling salted water ready and drop in the dumplings, a few at the time. They are ready as soon as they rise to the top.

Dry and place all the dumplings on a small baking tray. Cover them with grated cheese and bake for 10 minutes, finishing with 3-5 minutes under the grill to brown.

Leniwe
Lazy Dumplings

Serves 4–6

Leniwe are popular dumplings, and can be eaten in most Polish restaurants in the UK. They are called "lazy" because, unlike other Polish dumplings they are unfilled. This of course makes them easy to prepare. They resemble Italian *gnocchi*, although they are often smaller. In the recipe that follows, cheese and herbs are incorporated into the dough. *Leniwe* can be served just boiled, with some drizzled melted butter, or with fried bacon or mushrooms, or they can be sautéed with some strips of sun-dried tomatoes and sliced stoned olives.

250g (9oz) Polish white cheese (available from Polish delis), or use crumbled feta or cream cheese
$^1/_2$ tsp caster sugar
salt and pepper

1 egg, separated
3 tbsp finely chopped fresh thyme leaves
85g (3oz) potato flour
100g (3$^1/_2$oz) plain flour

Place the cheese in a mixing bowl and add the sugar, ½ tsp salt and the egg yolk. Mix well until everything has amalgamated together and the cheese is soft and creamy.

Add the thyme and some salt and pepper, and fold in the potato flour. Slowly add the plain flour, working the flour into the dough until it doesn't stick to your hands. Beat the egg white until just stiff, then fold it carefully into the cheese mixture. You should have a smooth and elastic dough.

Cut the dough in half, and make each half into a long, thin roll, about 1.5cm ($^1/_2$ inch) wide, like a frankfurter. Cut on the diagonal into small 2cm ($^3/_4$ inch) pieces.

Drop immediately into a large pot of boiling water to cook. *Leniwe* are ready when they have risen to the surface after 2-3 minutes of boiling. Drain well and serve (*see* above).

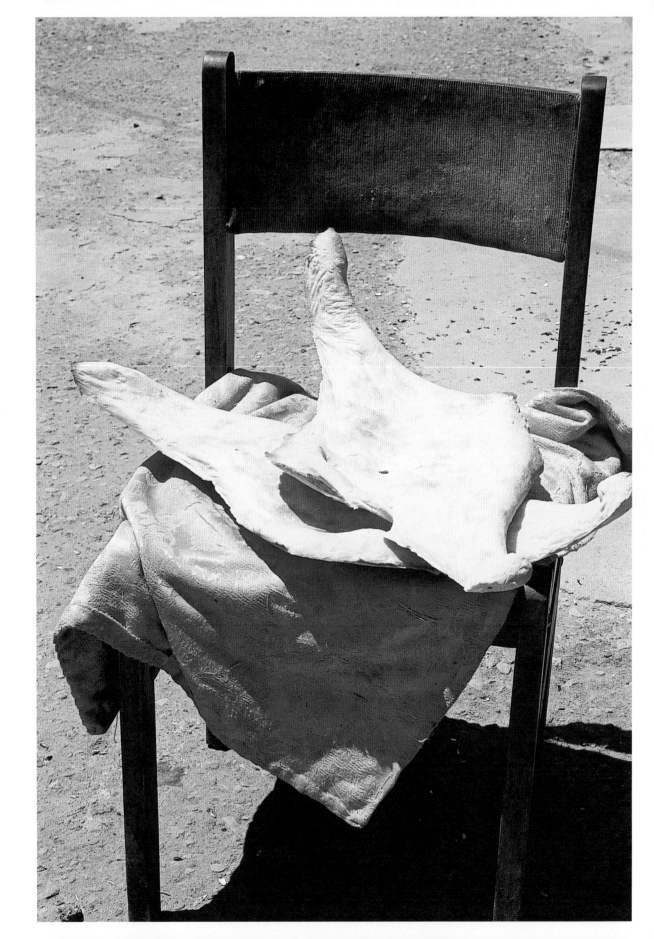

Potato Dumplings Sautéed with Feta and Capers

Serves 4–6

In Hungary they call these dumplings *doodle*. Their origins can be traced to Transylvania, where it is common to sauté dumplings in some butter or goose fat once they have been boiled.

200g (7oz) potatoes, peeled and grated
70g (2^{1}/$_{2}$oz) potato flour
salt and pepper
1 tbsp horseradish cream

1 tbsp goose fat or butter
150g (5^{1}/$_{2}$oz) sheep's milk feta cheese, cubed
2 tbsp capers, rinsed and chopped
1 tbsp chopped fresh parsley

Place the grated potatoes and potato flour in a large bowl and mix. Season with salt and pepper and mix in the horseradish cream.

Using your fingers, tear off small walnut-sized pieces of the mixture and drop them in a large pot of boiling salted water, a few at a time. Cook for about 10 minutes, or until they rise to the top of the water. Remove with a slotted spoon and place to drain.

In a heavy sauté pan, melt the fat or butter, add the dumplings, and stir them gently to brown on all sides. Add the cheese, capers and parsley and cook, stirring, for another 3-4 minutes. Serve hot.

Uszka
Polish Dumplings with Mushroom Filling

Makes 20–30

The Polish call them *uszka*, the Russians *ushki*; these are tiny dumplings. They're offered as an accompaniment to borscht or clear soup or served on their own.

85g (3oz) plain flour
salt and pepper
2 tbsp finely chopped fresh tarragon
1 egg yolk

Mushroom Filling
25g butter
1 small shallot, peeled and finely chopped
70g (2^{1}/$_{2}$oz) mushrooms, washed
    and finely chopped
1 egg white, lightly beaten
2 tbsp dried breadcrumbs

Make the dough by placing the flour in a bowl and adding salt and pepper to taste, the tarragon, egg yolk, and 2-3 tbsp water or more to mix it all to a dough.

Knead the dough on a floured board, then roll it out to approximately 1cm (^{1}/2 inch) thick and cut it into 5cm (2 inch) squares.

For the filling, melt the butter in a frying pan and sauté the shallot and mushrooms until soft. Season to taste and cool. Add half of the egg white and the breadcrumbs and mix again.

Brush the pastry squares with the remaining egg white, and spoon a little mushroom mixture on to the centre of each square. Fold so that each square makes a triangle, pinching the edges to seal.

Cook in plenty of boiling water for 3-4 minutes and drain.

Pierogi
Dumplings Filled with Cream Cheese, Potato and Chives
Serves 6

I grew up helping my grandmother in the kitchen, mixing batters, stuffing peppers and moulding pastry shapes while she would make the weekly batch of *pierogi*. She did that every week and then, once a month, she made her magic *baklava*. Her *pierogi* were crumbly and crispy on the outside and gooey and creamy on the inside.

Pierogi Dough
300g (10$^{1}/_{2}$oz) plain flour
2 eggs
salt and pepper
4-5 tbsp water

Cream Cheese Filling
2 large potatoes, boiled, skinned and mashed
200g (7oz) cream cheese
a bunch of spring onions, finely chopped
a bunch of fresh chives, finely chopped

To Serve
85g (3oz) butter
4 tsp sour cream

In a food processor, mix the flour, eggs, a pinch of salt and the water to get a smooth dough. Knead the dough on a floured board until it is smooth and elastic. Divide it in half and roll each half into a thin sheet on the floured board. Use a pasta machine if you have one. The dough should be the thickness of *ravioli*.

To make the filling, mix the mashed potato, cream cheese, spring onions and chives. Season.

Cut a sheet of dough into small rounds, about 6cm (2$^{1}/_{4}$ inch) in diameter, using a glass. Place a small spoonful of the filling on one half of each circle. Damp the edges with a little water. Fold over into a half-moon shape. Press the edges of the dough together using a fork or your fingers. Repeat until all the ingredients are used up.

To cook, boil a large pan of water and drop in the *pierogi* a few at a time. Boil, covered. When the *pierogi* rise to the top they are done. You can serve them with melted butter on top, which is traditional, or sauté them in the butter until they are browned. Serve with sour cream.

Pierogi with Sauerkraut, Mushrooms and Prunes

Serves 6

This recipe for *pierogi* is my favourite – even though it doesn't have the classic filling. Its secret is the use of butter and the slow braising.

1 recipe *pierogi* dough (*see* page 139)
sour cream

Filling
60g (2¼oz) butter
2 large onions, peeled and finely sliced
400g (14oz) sauerkraut, drained
400g (14oz) mushrooms, wiped and finely chopped
6 large prunes, stoned and finely chopped
salt and pepper

In a large saucepan, melt about a third of the butter over a slow heat and sauté the onions until almost golden in colour.

Meanwhile, wash the sauerkraut to make it less salty.

When the onion is soft and golden, add the mushrooms and another third of the butter. Braise slowly, stirring often, for about 20 minutes, until the mushrooms have softened.

Add the prunes and sauerkraut and the final third of butter, and continue cooking on a very low heat, mixing well, for another 20 minutes. Season with a little salt and pepper, remembering that the cabbage is already salty. The mixture is ready to use now.

Cut a sheet of dough into squares of approximately 6cm (2¼ inches). Arrange a spoonful of the filling along one edge of a piece of dough, 3cm (1¼ inch) from the edge. Damp the edges with a little water. Fold over into a triangle and cut into a semi-circle using a pastry cutter or glass. Press the edges of the dough together. Repeat with the rest until all the ingredients are used up.

To cook, boil a large pan of water and drop in the *pierogi* a few at a time. Boil, covered. When the *pierogi* rise to the top they are done. You can serve them simply with melted butter on top, which is the traditional way, or sauté them in the butter until they are lightly browned. Serve the *pierogi* with sour cream.

Potato Croquettes

Makes 10–12

This is one of my father's specialties. Every now and again he would make these fancy potato dumplings as an accompaniment. Croquettes are popular in most Eastern European cuisines, not only in Bulgaria. Hungarians are great masters of potato croquettes. A croquette is usually a small savoury or sweet preparation. The most common shape of croquettes is cork-like, but they can be ball-shaped. They are usually coated with breadcrumbs and offered as a starter or canapé.

5 slices white bread, toasted (for breadcrumbs)
6 large potatoes, peeled
salt and pepper

4 egg yolks
$^1/_4$ tsp freshly grated nutmeg
vegetable oil for deep-frying

To make the breadcrumbs, place the toasted bread in a food processor and whizz until fine. Put them on a plate.

Cook the potatoes in boiling salted water until tender. Drain and put them through a potato ricer, or mash them by hand until very smooth. Add the egg yolks and nutmeg and season with salt and pepper, mixing well.

Form the potato dough into 10-12 small corks, about 3cm ($1^1/_4$ inch) long, and roll in the breadcrumbs until they are coated.

Have your vegetable oil heated up to almost boiling point. Drop the croquettes in, a few at a time, and fry for about 3-4 minutes, until crisp and browned. Drain on kitchen paper. Serve hot.

Vareniky
Ukrainian Dumplings Stuffed with Spring Onion and Chicken Liver
Serves 4–6

Borscht and *vareniky* are two of the most famous Ukrainian dishes. *Vareniky* are offered in just about every home in the Ukraine when a guest is visiting and are always freshly homemade. The recipe below is prepared with a rather rich dough, making these *vareniky* particularly delicious. Ukrainians always prepare *vareniky* in vast quantities – there is an old superstition that if *vareniky* are counted, the dough will split and the filling will spill out. Serve these with sour cream.

200g (7oz) plain flour
a generous pinch of salt
3 eggs
2 tsp melted butter

300g (10¹⁄₂oz) fresh chicken livers, trimmed and finely chopped
salt and pepper
3 tbsp chopped fresh thyme leaves

Filling
8 spring onions, washed and finely chopped
2 tbsp olive oil

To Serve
100g (3¹⁄₂oz) bacon, finely cubed
4 tbsp melted butter
sour cream

To make the dough, place the flour and salt in a large mixing bowl and make a well in the centre. Beat 2 of the eggs, and add them to the well along with the melted butter. Mix everything to an elastic and smooth dough, and then knead on a floured work surface for about 5 minutes. Wrap in clingfilm and chill in the fridge for 30 minutes.

Meanwhile, for the filling, sauté the onions in the olive oil until slightly transparent but not browned, about 3-4 minutes. Add the chicken livers and cook for a further 2 minutes. Season with salt and pepper and add the thyme. Mix well and keep until ready to use.

Take the dough out of the fridge and rest at room temperature for 15 minutes. Roll the dough to about 3-4mm thick and then, using a cup about 5cm (2 inches) in diameter, cut out as many rounds as you can. Spoon a tsp of the liver and spring onion mixture into the middle of each pastry round, and brush the edges of the pastry with the remaining beaten egg. Fold in half-moon shapes and press the edges gently with your fingers at first, then slightly harder, using a fork, to seal.

Drop the *vareniky*, a few at a time, into a large pan of gently simmering water, and cook for about 5 minutes. Drain with a slotted spoon and keep warm while you cook the rest.

Put the bacon into a heavy sauté pan, and sauté in its own fat until crisp. Add the *vareniky* and butter. Mix well and serve immediately with sour cream.

Pirozhki
Russian Dumplings

Makes about 40–50

This is a rather special recipe. Just as I like to make my *blini* with a sour-cream dough, these *pirozhki* also have a sour-cream dough. The result is a crumbly, flaky and somewhat tart pastry. *Pirozhki* are a national favourite and, unlike *pierogi* or *vareniky,* they are always baked.

Sour-Cream Pastry	*Chicken Filling*
225g (8oz) plain flour	1 onion, peeled and finely chopped
$1/2$ tsp salt	4 tbsp vegetable oil
$1/2$ tsp baking powder	200g (7oz) minced chicken
100g ($3^1/2$oz) butter, chilled and cubed	$1/2$ small bunch fresh parsley, finely chopped
2 large egg yolks, beaten	salt and pepper
125ml (4fl oz) sour cream	2 egg yolks, beaten

For the filling, sauté the onion in the oil in a heavy frying pan until soft and transparent, about 3 minutes. Add the chicken mince and cook for 10 more minutes. Stir in the parsley and season with salt and pepper. Cool until ready to use.

To make the sour-cream pastry, place the flour, salt and baking powder in a large mixing bowl. Add the butter cubes and, using your fingers, mix it all together, rubbing the butter into the flour until it resembles breadcrumbs.

Add the beaten egg yolks and sour cream to the pastry a little at a time, working it all together to achieve a smooth and elastic pastry. Knead for 2-3 minutes, then wrap in clingfilm and refrigerate for an hour.

Preheat the oven to 190ºC/375ºF/gas mark 5.

When ready to make the *pirozhki,* roll out half the dough to about 3-4mm thick. Using a pastry cutter or a glass about 8cm (3 inches) in diameter, stamp out as many rounds as you can.

Brush the edges of the pastry rounds with beaten egg yolk, and place a spoonful of filling in the middle of each. Press the edges gently together to make a half-moon shape. Repeat with the rest of the dough and filling.

Place the *pirozhki* on a baking sheet, brush the tops with egg yolk, and bake for 25 minutes.

butter week
DAIRY

They cherished in their peaceful life

The precious old ways of former days:

When Shrovetide came, they offered their guests

Butter pancakes in quaint country ways.

Eugene Onegin (a novel in verse), *Complete Collected Works in 6 Tomes,* Alexander Pushkin[8]

The original bacteria strain for yoghurt is said to be *thermobacterium bulgaricum* – Bulgarian yoghurt, which has been made for centuries right across the Balkans. To this day, yoghurt plays a major role in the diet of most Bulgarians. It is to this yoghurt bacterium, which is referred to as the "bacillus of life", that the longevity of Bulgarian people is credited. Many tales have been told through the centuries of ordinary country folk who have lived to see a hundred summers and more.

The Bulgarians and Georgians are steeped in an almost folkloric tradition of using home-made yoghurts, yoghurt drinks and all manner of cheeses made from goat's, cow's and sheep's milk on a daily basis. For instance, a soft, feta-style curd cheese, custom-made from either sheep's or goat's milk, is prepared all over the region and, unpasteurized, it is stored in brine until ready to use. This tangy, salty cheese is used extensively in the homely recipes of many countries and, along with yoghurt, it appears in many baked dishes, both sweet and savoury.

For the Slavic people, food has always been highly symbolic. The ancients worshipped the sun, honouring it by cooking and eating its image in the form of thin, round cakes, much the same as *blini.* (I have given what I find to be the most delicious and delectable of *blini* recipes in the first chapter of the book because *blini* are the usual suspect on the *zakuska* table.) In Russia an elaborate and indulgent "Butter Week" festival is still held to celebrate the arrival of spring.

Peppers Stuffed with Feta and Mint

Serves 4

This is one of the most memorable dishes of my childhood. As soon as the sweet red peppers were in season and at their cheapest, my mother would start preparing this dish. We would buy 20-30 kilos and preserve them for the winter months, when my mum would prepare the same dish, bringing summer flavours to the table in the midst of a deep, cold winter.

8 red peppers
300g (10$^{1}/_{2}$oz) sheep's milk feta, crumbled
2 eggs
1 tbsp Quark

a large handful of chopped fresh mint
salt and pepper
1 tbsp plain flour
5 tbsp olive oil

Place the peppers on a skewer or long fork, directly on the flame of your gas cooker hob, and cook, turning to blacken the skin evenly. If you have an electric cooker, place the peppers under the grill, 2-3 peppers at a time, and turn them around in the same way.

When the skin has blackened all over, remove the peppers and place in a plastic bag. Leave to cool; this will help you remove the burned skin. As soon as the peppers are cool enough to handle, peel them and carefully remove their stalks and seeds, keeping the peppers whole. The flesh of the peppers will be soft and slightly slippery. Keep aside until ready to stuff.

In a large mixing bowl, place the feta cheese, eggs, Quark and mint and season with salt and pepper. Mix well with a fork.

To stuff the peppers, carefully spoon in a little of filling with a small spoon. Dust the peppers with some flour.

In a heavy non-stick pan, heat the olive oil, and sauté the peppers until golden brown all over, about 3-5 minutes on each side. Serve warm or cold.

Lithuanian Carrot Baba

Serves 6

This is the Lithuanian vegetable *baba* (as in yeast *baba* cake). It is a rather elegant way of preparing almost any kind of root vegetable. The recipe originates in Lithuania, but I had it prepared by Isak Katzen in Maryland in the United States on my last trip there. The original had smoked fish added.

85g (3oz) butter
2 tbsp olive oil
3 shallots, peeled and finely chopped
800g (1lb 12oz) carrots, peeled and grated
2 apples, peeled, cored and grated
50g (1³/₄oz) golden sultanas
150ml (5fl oz) sour cream

1 large egg yolk, beaten
1 tsp clear honey
¹/₄ tsp ground coriander
¹/₄ tsp ground cumin
salt and pepper
150g (5¹/₂oz) brioche breadcrumbs

Preheat the oven to 180°C/350°F/gas mark 4.

In a large non-stick pan, melt 20g of the butter and the olive oil and cook the shallots until soft. Add the carrot, apple and sultanas, and continue cooking for another 5-7 minutes, stirring all the time. Remove from the heat. Butter a medium baking tray and pour in the carrot mixture.

In a small, heavy based saucepan, melt 50g butter. Remove from the heat and allow to cool a little. In a mixing bowl, mix the sour cream, melted butter, egg yolk, honey, coriander and cumin together. Season with salt and pepper. Pour this beaten mixture over the carrot mixture in the baking tray.

In a separate small frying pan, brown the brioche breadcrumbs in a little more butter for about 2 minutes. Sprinkle on top of the carrot and sour cream mixture and bake for 25-30 minutes, until golden brown.

Aubergine Rolls Stuffed with Feta Cheese and Basil

Serves 4

This is a favourite in my father's aubergine repertoire. Today he is still the king of cooking with aubergines. He has a special touch and his imagination is truly fired when he prepares aubergines. He would normally use white aubergines in this recipe, which have a particularly milky and mellow flesh, but fresh purple aubergines work well too, especially if they were bought in an Italian or Turkish shop.

2 aubergines, sliced lengthwise into
   12 thin slices
salt and pepper
150g (5$^{1}/_{2}$oz) plain flour
3 eggs, beaten
150g (5$^{1}/_{2}$oz) fine brioche breadcrumbs
150g (5$^{1}/_{2}$oz) Parmesan, finely grated

200g (7oz) sheep's milk feta cheese, grated
100g (3$^{1}/_{2}$oz) mild Cheddar, coarsely grated
a small bunch of fresh basil, chopped

To Serve
200g (7oz) freshly cooked tomato sauce (good-
   quality shop-bought, or your usual pasta sauce)

Preheat the oven to 180°C/350°F/gas mark 4. Oil 2 large baking sheets.

Season the aubergine slices with salt and pepper. Place the flour in a shallow plate, the eggs in another, and mix the breadcrumbs and two-thirds of the Parmesan in a third. Coat each of the aubergine slices with flour, then dip in the beaten egg and finally coat them with the breadcrumb/Parmesan mixture. Lay the aubergine slices on the prepared baking trays and bake in the preheated oven for 20-30 minutes, turning them halfway through the cooking time. Allow to cool a little before stuffing.

Mix the feta, Cheddar and basil, and season with a little salt and pepper.

Divide the cheese mixture among the baked aubergine slices, spreading it evenly. Roll each slice by starting from one short end, enclosing the filling.

Arrange the rolls, seam-side down, on a baking dish, and spoon some tomato sauce over them. Sprinkle with the remaining Parmesan and bake for 20 minutes. Serve hot.

Stuffed Baby Aubergines

Serves 4

This is my father's favourite dish and, after years of practice, he has got it down to a work of art. He still prepares it for the most special of occasions. Bulgarian aubergines have a very light, soft flesh, without any bitterness. I find that if I use young, milky, tender aubergines, I get a really good result. Cooking an aubergine can be very tricky, but get it right and it is delectable. You will notice the slight Turkish overtones in this recipe, which is not unusual for Bulgaria: the Turks dominated the region for more than 500 years.

16 baby aubergines
6 tbsp extra-virgin olive oil
1 onion, peeled and finely chopped
3 garlic cloves, peeled and crushed
2 large tomatoes, finely chopped

2 red peppers, roasted, peeled and chopped
$1/2$ tsp ground cumin
salt and pepper
$1/2$ bunch fresh parsley, chopped
200ml (7fl oz) strained yogurt, to serve

Halve the baby aubergines lengthwise along the centre, through the stalks. Scoop out the flesh of each half, leaving a casing of about 2cm ($3/4$ inch) of flesh.

Place a large non-stick pan on a medium heat and heat 4 tbsp of the oil until hot and smoking. Sauté a few aubergine halves at a time for about 3-4 minutes on each side, until golden brown, and remove to a baking tray, flesh-side up. Repeat with all the aubergine halves.

Meanwhile, finely chop the flesh scooped from the aubergines and keep to one side.

Preheat the oven to 200°C/400°F/gas mark 6.

In another medium non-stick pan, heat the remaining oil and gently sauté the onion and garlic over a very low heat until just softened and golden brown, for about 3-4 minutes. Add the chopped aubergine flesh, the tomato, peppers and cumin, and season to taste. Continue to cook on the low heat for a further 15 minutes, stirring frequently. Add the parsley.

Fill the aubergine halves with the filling, piling it high. Bake for 15 minutes, until the tops are golden brown. Serve hot with a dollop of yoghurt.

Feta, Pumpkin and Spinach Tart

Serves 4

An easy open-top tart, made with filo pastry. I have amended it slightly, so it is not quite as it is made in Bulgaria.

5 tbsp melted butter	***Filling***
200g (7oz) fresh filo pastry	**300g (10^1/$_2$oz) fresh spinach, washed**
20ml olive oil	**2 large eggs**
100g (3^1/$_2$oz) shelled almonds, freshly ground	**200g (7oz) cooked pumpkin flesh, cubed**
	150g (5^1/$_2$oz) sheep's milk feta, crumbled
	150g (5^1/$_2$oz) mild Cheddar, grated
	salt and pepper

Preheat the oven to 200ºC/400ºF/gas mark 6. Lightly brush a rectangular tart pan with a little of the melted butter (if you do not have such a pan, use a baking sheet or a Swiss roll tin instead).

To make the filling, cook the spinach in a large pan with 2 tbsp water, stirring until the leaves have wilted, about 2 minutes. Cool.

In a large bowl, whisk the eggs. Add the cooled spinach, the pumpkin and cheeses. Mix well, and season with salt and pepper.

Place the filo sheets on a work surface, covering those you are not using immediately with clingfilm and a damp kitchen towel to prevent the pastry from drying. Combine the oil with the remaining melted butter. Lightly brush 1 sheet with the oil and butter and sprinkle with some of the ground almonds. Repeat in the same way, layering with 6 more filo sheets, and more butter and almonds. Transfer those sheets to the baking tray and let them hang over the sides.

Spoon the spinach and cheese mixture on top, and spread evenly. Fold the edges of the filo over the filling about 5cm (2 inches), leaving a small rectangle in the centre uncovered. Lightly brush the top with melted butter and sprinkle with ground almonds.

Bake for 25 minutes, until the pastry is golden and crisp. Serve warm.

Vita Banitza
Courgette and Feta Filo Pie

Serves 6

There has never been a Christmas in my house without *banitza*. It is traditionally prepared for Christmas Eve as part of a vegetarian menu. My grandmother use to make the very best *banitza:* it was in her hands, she used to say. She gave the recipe to all who asked for it, but no one could ever master it as she could, so she concluded that the secret lay in her hands! *Banitza* is prepared using filo pastry, which is the most common pastry in Bulgaria. The courgette filling is a specialty of the northern part of the country.

400g (14oz) filo pastry
50g (1³/₄oz) butter, melted
1 tsp caraway seeds

Filling
2 tsp olive oil
1 small onion, peeled and diced
400g (14oz) courgettes, unpeeled, diced
200g (7oz) sheep's milk feta, crumbled
2 eggs, beaten
1 bunch fresh dill, finely chopped

Preheat the oven to 180°C/350°F/gas mark 4. Have ready a large, round baking tray, about 20-24cm (8-10 inches) in diameter.

For the filling, heat the olive oil in a frying pan. Add the onion and courgettes and cook for 3-4 minutes. Transfer the mixture to a large mixing bowl and leave to cool. Add the feta, eggs and dill and mix well.

Lay 2 filo sheets on a work surface and cover the rest with a damp cloth. Brush a sheet with some butter, top with the other sheet and spoon about 2 tbsp of filling along the long edge (filo sheets are rectangular), leaving 2cm (³/₄ inch) on each side, folding in the ends and rolling the pastry up over the filling. Repeat with the remaining filo sheets and filling.

Form the pastry rolls into a large spiral shape by firmly coiling them around each other in the round baking tray. Brush the tops generously with melted butter and sprinkle with caraway seeds. Bake for 30-40 minutes, until the pastry is golden brown. Serve cooled.

Khachapuri
Georgian Bread

Makes 8

Khachapuri is a cheese bread that is presented to guests when they visit a Georgian home, offered just baked and piping hot; it is what Georgians consider to be fast food. *Khachapuri* comes in diverse shapes and a variety of cheeses are used to stuff it, depending on where in Georgia it is made. The most common form is *suluguni,* made using home-produced sheep's-milk cheese, and the dough is tenderized by the addition of *matsoni* or yoghurt. This recipe was given to me by Neli Guledani from Gamadgveba, a small village near Tbilisi. I visited her unannounced, but she immediately made up a batch of her *khachapuri* for me. We sat outside in the warm sunshine and enjoyed this most delicious and satisfying of breads.

500ml (18fl oz) *matsoni* or yoghurt
1 egg yolk
$^1/_2$ tbsp caster sugar
$^1/_2$ tsp salt
600g (1lb 5oz) plain flour

$1^1/_2$ tbsp baking powder
500g (1lb 2oz) soft cheese, eg Danish Havarti
1 egg, beaten
salt and pepper
3 tbsp melted butter

For the basic dough, place the yoghurt in a medium mixing bowl and add the egg yolk, sugar and salt. Mix well, then slowly stir in the flour and baking powder, mixing all the time until a smooth dough forms. Add more flour if the dough is sticky. Leave to rise for at least an hour.

Crumble or grate the cheese and put it in a bowl. Beat in the egg, then season.

Preheat the oven to 200°C/400°F/gas mark 6, and grease a baking tray.

Divide the dough into 8 pieces and, working with 1 piece at a time, roll out on a lightly floured surface into 12cm (5 inch) rounds.

Place $1^1/_2$ tbsp of the cheese mixture in the centre of each round, then gather the sides up and twist the tops to seal. Gently roll on a floured surface into 15cm (6 inch) rounds. Repeat with all the dough as above.

Place on the prepared baking tray and bake for 10-15 minutes. While still hot, brush generously with melted butter and serve. *Khachapuri* is best eaten piping-hot.

Lentil and Feta Salad with Sour Cream Pesto

Serves 4

Lentils are, for me, a must. They are used in many Eastern European countries and are commonly added to soups, stews and salads. The Hungarians dearly love lentils and find them irresistible when served slightly soured. This recipe is a *mélange* of various dishes, a slightly sour version of a lentil salad given to me by my Jewish friend Andrea. I have added a creamy pesto.

10g (^{1}/4oz) butter
1 shallot, peeled and chopped
1 carrot, peeled and chopped
500g (1lb 2oz) puy lentils
a handful of fresh parsley, celery and thyme
    leaves
juice of 2 lemons
4 tbsp extra-virgin olive oil
^{1}/2 tsp sweet paprika
200g (7oz) sheep's milk feta, cubed

Sour Cream Pesto
125g (4^{1}/2oz) ground almonds
250ml (9fl oz) sour cream
2 garlic cloves, peeled and crushed
^{1}/2 bunch fresh parsley leaves
^{1}/2 bunch fresh mint leaves
juice of 1 lemon
40ml (1^{1}/2fl oz) extra-virgin olive oil
salt and pepper

Make the pesto by placing the almonds, sour cream, garlic and herbs in a food processor. Process until well combined, then add the lemon juice and olive oil while the motor is still running. Season to taste.

Melt the butter in a large saucepan. Add the shallot and carrot and sauté for 2 minutes. Add the lentils, herbs and 250ml of water, or enough to cover the lentils. Bring to the boil and then simmer until the lentils are cooked, about 15 minutes. Drain and discard the herbs.

Add the lemon juice and olive oil, and season with salt, pepper and the paprika. Mix well and add the feta cheese. Serve the salad with some sour cream pesto.

Chicken Baked in Yoghurt

Serves 4

Two-thirds of Bulgaria's total milk production is converted into yoghurt. They don't make the fruit-flavoured stuff; it is all plain and very refreshing. One particular type is called *katuk*. The milk is thickened by protracted simmering, then poured into sheep-skin bags and allowed to cool. This yoghurt is stored for the winter under a protective layer of sheep's butter.

2 tbsp olive oil

2 large onions, peeled and sliced

4 large chicken breasts, bone in, halved

1kg (2lb 4oz) thick yoghurt, made from Ω
  sheep's milk (or use Greek yoghurt)

2 eggs, beaten

2 tbsp plain flour

4 tbsp chopped fresh mint

$^1/_2$ tsp ground cumin

3 garlic cloves, peeled and crushed

salt and pepper

Preheat the oven to 180°C/350°F/gas mark 4.

Heat the oil in a heavy ovenproof sauté pan and fry the onions until soft. Remove. Add the chicken pieces to the oil and cook for about 5-6 minutes, turning them around to brown evenly. Return the onions to the pan and stir to mix well.

In a separate bowl, mix the thick yoghurt, eggs, flour, mint, cumin and garlic. Stir really well and season with salt and pepper. Pour the yoghurt mixture over the chicken and sautéed onions and place in the oven.

Cook for 40-50 minutes, until the yoghurt has set and has become slightly brown on top and the chicken is cooked through. (The yoghurt sets a little like custard.) Serve hot with boiled rice.

Bulgarian Yoghurt and Meatball Soup

Serves 4–6

This is another dish from my home country and, as in the previous recipe, our neighbours, the Turks, have heavily influenced it. It also has Jewish overtones, there being a rather large Jewish community in Bulgaria, especially in my home town of Plovdiv. This hearty soup is a favourite with all children back home, a whole meal in one pot. The meatballs are cooked in the soup broth, instead of being browned separately as is usually the case with meatballs.

1 litre (1³/₄ pints) chicken stock
2 large potatoes, peeled and grated
1 large carrot, peeled and grated
3 tbsp plain yoghurt
1 egg yolk
2 tbsp lemon juice
3 tbsp finely chopped fresh parsley

Meatballs
200g (7oz) veal mince
200g (7oz) pork mince
1 large slice crusty bread, crusts discarded,
    soaked in water and squeezed dry
¹/₂ medium onion, finely chopped
salt and pepper
1 tbsp plain flour

In a large bowl, combine the veal and pork, the bread and onion. Season to taste and mix well until the mixture holds together. Shape into small meatballs, about 2cm (³/₄ inch) in diameter. Roll in the plain flour and shake off the excess.

Bring the chicken or veal stock to the boil in a large saucepan. Drop the meatballs in, along with the grated potato and carrot. Simmer for about 20 minutes until the meatballs are cooked.

Meanwhile, in a small bowl mix the plain yoghurt, egg yolk and lemon juice. Add some of the soup liquid to this, then return the mixture to the pot of soup. Mix well, heat through briefly, and sprinkle with parsley.

Kyufteta Baked in Yoghurt

Serves 6–8

This is sometimes called "yoghurt *gyuvech* with meatballs", a famous dish from the western part of Bulgaria. I was fortunate enough to be taught to make this dish by an elderly monk living in a small, remote monastery in the mountains. I must admit that I never had this as a child, but am certainly making up for lost time now. *Kyufte* is a small meatball and it is very common in Bulgaria, part of everyday meals and a favourite street food. It takes many years of experience to make a really mean *kyufte*! Here is my father's recipe, tried and tested almost daily.

a little milk

2 slices white bread

1 small onion, peeled and finely chopped

$^1/_2$ bunch fresh parsley, finely chopped

1 egg

450g (1lb) mixed pork and veal mince

salt and pepper

3 tbsp plain flour

3-4 tbsp olive oil

Yoghurt Mixture

3 eggs

400g (14oz) thick yoghurt (Greek-style)

Preheat the oven to 180°C/350°F/gas mark 4.

Place the milk in a medium bowl and add the bread to soak. Squeeze out any excess liquid and place the bread in a large mixing bowl. Add the onion, parsley, egg and minced meats, and mix thoroughly. Season with salt and pepper. With dampened hands, form small, golf-ball-sized meatballs. Slightly flatten them, then coat with flour.

Heat the oil in a large frying pan over a medium heat, then cook the meatballs for 3-4 minutes on each side. Arrange them in a shallow earthenware dish.

To make the yoghurt mixture, beat the eggs with some salt and pepper. Gradually add the yoghurt and pour it over the *kyufteta* in the dish, making sure that only the tops of the *kyufteta* are visible.

Bake for 45 minutes, until golden brown on top.

THE BOYAR TABLE

The spray of "Comet" fine Champagne,

The sweet and tender hunters' roast,

And truffles, too – the gourmand's choice

O, the delights of the French cuisine!

Divine, imported Strasbourg pies,

A sliver of Limburg cheese

And pineapple from overseas.

Eugene Onegin (a novel in verse), *Complete Collected Works in 6 Tomes*, Alexander Pushkin[9]

It would have been impossible to write about the people and food of Eastern Europe without devoting a chapter to the era of grand and classical cuisine, the era of the boyars and tsars. That food was important is well-known. What food represented – the giving of life and the preservation of the soul – has been immortalized by Pushkin, Gogol, Dostoevsky, Tolstoy and Chekov in their colossal works. But this was also a time when tsar, prince and boyar turned their cultural gaze upon the sophistication of the grand western European cuisine, that of the French, the Austrians and the rest. It was the nobility that brought top western European chefs of the day to the courts of the Russian tsars, Polish kings and Magyar *kiraly* (*kirai*), and it was they who commissioned the classic dishes we still know so well: chicken Kiev, beef Stroganoff, veal Orloff, *dobos torte* and strudel.

Few good things came out of the isolation that Communism brought, but undoubtedly one benefit that we can now reap is that the foundations of the national cuisines were never adulterated by the changes in culinary fashions that swept across Europe during those years.

Polish, Hungarian and Russian cooking had their heyday during the late nineteenth century in the homes of the nobility, when amazing dishes were created by distinguished French and Swiss chefs, hired by the aristocratic boyars of the day. Dishes like salad Olivier (*see* page 174), beef Stroganoff, pheasant *souvorov*, Hussar's roast, Madame Rose crayfish bisque and many more were created to flatter and enhance the egos of the wealthy and noble society. These classic dishes were based on French cuisine, and these foundations brought refinement and finesse to much of the cuisine of Russia, Hungary and Poland.

Baltic Stuffed Potatoes

Serves 6

These days, the fashionable restaurants of London and New York abound with dishes made with wild mushrooms. But in countries such as Lithuania, Bulgaria and Russia, the picking of mushrooms was, and still is, a national pastime. Children from a very young age are taught to recognize the different varieties, and know their names and the uses to which they can be put.

3 large baking potatoes, washed and dried
salt and pepper
20g (^{3}/₄oz) butter
4 shallots, peeled and finely chopped
2 garlic cloves, peeled and crushed

200g (7oz) mixed wild mushrooms, wiped
 and dried
100ml (3^1/₂fl oz) sour cream
3 tsp finely chopped fresh tarragon

Preheat the oven to 180°C/350°F/gas mark 4.

Pierce the potatoes and bake them for 1-1^1/₂ hours, or until cooked. Remove from the oven. When cool enough to handle, halve them and scoop the potato flesh out into a bowl, leaving 2cm (^{3}/₄ inch) shells. Season the shells with salt and pepper and keep to one side.

In a small sauté pan, melt the butter and fry the shallots, garlic and mushrooms until slightly coloured, about 10 minutes.

Mash the potato pulp well, adding the sautéed mushrooms, sour cream and tarragon. Season to taste and mix thoroughly.

Stuff the mixture back into the potato shells, piling it high. Bake in the same hot-temperature oven until the potatoes are golden in colour, about 15-20 minutes.

Olivier Salad

Serves 6

Olivier, who was the French chef of Czar Nicholas II, created this salad in the second half of the nineteenth century. Just like Caesar salad, Olivier salad comes in many forms, and you can easily be put off if you've had one that was badly prepared. It is also known simply as Russian salad, and I have never had a better one than my mother's. She was famous in our neighbourhood for it, and she still makes it for special occasions.

200g (7oz) cooked ham, diced
3 frankfurters, sliced
1 large potato, boiled, peeled and diced
1 large carrot, boiled, peeled and diced
100g (3^{1}/$_{2}$oz) peas, cooked
2 medium gherkins, diced
2 eggs, hard-boiled, shelled and diced
50g (1^{3}/$_{4}$oz) green beans, cooked and chopped
^{1}/$_{2}$ tbsp Dijon mustard
salt and pepper
2 tbsp chopped fresh parsley

Mayonnaise
1 egg
1 hard-boiled egg yolk
150ml (5fl oz) olive oil
2 tbsp lemon juice

To prepare the mayonnaise, in a food processor combine the raw egg and cooked egg yolk, season with salt and pepper and blend well. With the motor running, start to add a fine stream of olive oil. Here you need patience, as you must add the oil very slowly. If you are too quick, the consistency will be more like a sauce than a thick creamy mayonnaise. Add the lemon juice and keep in the fridge until needed.

In a large bowl, mix the ham, frankfurters, potato, carrot, peas, gherkins, eggs, beans and mustard, and season to taste. Add about 4 tbsp mayonnaise and mix, making sure that you don't crush the vegetables too much. Add the parsley and serve.

Bagration Salad

Serves 6

This salad was prepared as part of the celebrations for what was considered to be the victory of Major General Prince Bagration and his troops over Napoleon at Eylau. There are also recipes for Bagration eggs, Bagration soup and Bagration timbales....

200g (7oz) macaroni

250g (9oz) chicken breast, boiled and skinned

150g (5^1/$_2$oz) frankfurters, cubed

2 Granny Smith apples, cored and chopped into bite-sized pieces

100g (3^1/$_2$oz) fresh podded peas, blanched

10 black olives, stoned and chopped

2 large hard-boiled eggs, shelled and chopped

5 tbsp mayonnaise (*see* page 174)

2 tbsp sour cream

salt and pepper

juice of 1 lemon

4 tbsp chopped fresh dill

Boil the macaroni in water until soft, then drain. Chop the chicken breasts and mix with the frankfurters in a large bowl, then add the apple, peas, olives and eggs and mix again.

Put the mayonnaise in a small bowl and add the sour cream. Season to taste and pour over the salad, adding the macaroni as well. Stir in the lemon juice and dill. Serve cold.

Pozharsky Kotleti
Chicken Croquettes

Serves 4–6

On the road from Moscow to St Petersburg lies the small wayside town of Torzhok, and it was here, in the early part of the nineteenth century, that Alexander Pushkin wrote to a friend and suggested that the best *pozharsky kotleti* could be had at the Pozharsky Tavern, and he should pay a visit next time he was passing. Who am I to argue with the great man? But the best *pozharsky kotleti* I have eaten was at the Pushkin Café, possibly the finest restaurant that Moscow has to offer. Alex Zaitsev, the general manager there, explained to me how *pozharsky kotleti* came to be. Legend has it that when Tsar Alexander was travelling on the road between the two cities, he decided to stop for lunch at a little inn, the Pozharsky Tavern. The tsar ordered veal cutlets. Pozharsky was panic-stricken as he had run out of veal but, thinking on his feet, he decided that he had to create an alternative dish. He prepared fluffy and delicate chicken and partridge croquettes, gently rolled them in fine breadcrumbs and fried them in pure butter. The tsar was thrilled with the dish and Pozharsky, encouraged, admitted to his trick. The tsar did not reprimand him for his fraud, but rewarded him with a medal and put *pozharsky kotleti* on the royal menu.

2 slices medium-sliced white bread	salt and pepper
100ml (3½fl oz) double cream	600g (1lb 5oz) veal mince
1 egg yolk	250g (9oz) chicken mince
2 tbsp Madeira	250g (9oz) fine brioche crumbs
2 tbsp finely chopped fresh dill	100g (3½oz) clarified butter

Soak the bread in the cream, then squeeze it almost dry and discard the excess cream. Place the bread in a large mixing bowl, add the egg yolk, Madeira and dill, and season with salt and pepper. Mix well, then mix in the veal and chicken mince.

Mould the mixture into oval croquettes, about 3cm (1¼ inches) thick and 5cm (2 inches) wide – you should have between 8 and 12, depending on the size you make them. Coat well in brioche crumbs and fry gently in the clarified butter on a low-to-medium heat for about 5-6 minutes on each side, until cooked through.

This dish is traditionally served with a mushroom and sour cream sauce.

Chicken Satsivi

Serves 4

This is a classic Georgian dish. Georgian cuisine is famed for its nut sauces, and *satsivi,* made with walnuts, is the most popular one. This dish is usually offered either cold or warm. *Satsivi* can accompany fish or vegetables as well as chicken or turkey. The quality of the walnuts is crucial for the taste of the sauce. I had it prepared in the home of Molly Zubelashvilli who, when it comes to Georgian Jewish cooking, has no equal in her ability to offer immense legendary feasts. Jews have lived in Georgia for well over two millennia, and although many have emigrated to the United States, the Jewish influence in Georgia is still visible.

10g (¼oz) butter
1 tbsp vegetable oil
4 chicken breasts, skinned and boned
salt and pepper

Satsivi Sauce
25g (1oz) butter
1 large onion, peeled and finely chopped
300g (10½oz) fresh shelled walnuts

a small bunch of fresh coriander, chopped
4 garlic cloves, peeled and chopped
1 small dried chilli pepper
1 tsp powdered cinnamon
1 tsp powdered marigold or saffron
½ tsp sweet paprika
175ml (6fl oz) chicken stock
60ml (2¼fl oz) white-wine vinegar

To make the sauce, melt the butter in a heavy non-stick pan and sauté the onion until soft and transparent. Place the walnuts, coriander, garlic and chilli pepper in a food processor and process to a paste. Add the sautéed onion and process further.

Place the paste back in the heavy non-stick pan over a low heat and add the cinnamon, marigold and paprika, mixing well. Season with salt and pepper. Gradually stir in the chicken stock and finally stir in the vinegar. Continue cooking until the sauce has slightly thickened – about 25 more minutes. If you would like the sauce to be thicker then you could use about ½ tbsp plain flour to thicken it.

To cook the chicken, melt the butter in a frying pan and add the oil. Add the chicken breasts and brown on both sides, seasoning with salt and pepper. Reduce the heat and cook slowly for another 15 minutes, turning halfway through, until the chicken is cooked through. Let the chicken cool.

Slice the chicken breasts diagonally and arrange on a large platter. Pour over the *satsivi* sauce.

Chicken Imereti

Serves 4

Of all the Georgian dishes, this is my favourite. It comes from the province of Imereti in central Georgia, not far from the city of Tbilisi. It is a kind of light stew, made with fresh garlic, plenty of fragrant, freshly ground *shafran,* or dry marigold, cumin and walnuts. Serve with a rice pilaf.

1 chicken, about 1.2kg (2lb 11oz)	1 dried red chilli pepper
3 tbsp vegetable oil	1 tbsp powdered marigold or crumbled saffron
salt and pepper	1 tsp ground cumin
2 large onions, peeled and finely sliced	50ml (2fl oz) white wine vinegar
200g (7oz) fresh shelled walnuts	300ml (10fl oz) chicken stock
8 garlic cloves, peeled	

Cut the chicken into 8 pieces. Heat the oil in a heavy casserole dish over a medium-to-high heat. Sauté the chicken pieces, a few at a time, making sure that they are evenly browned all over. Season with salt and pepper. Remove to a separate plate with a slotted spoon

Add the onions to the oil in the pan and braise until soft and transparent, for 6 minutes, stirring all the time.

Meanwhile, place the walnuts, garlic, chilli pepper, marigold and cumin in the food processor and process to a dryish paste. Add the vinegar slowly and mix to a smooth paste.

Return the chicken to the onions and add the walnut paste, mixing well. Slowly add the chicken stock, cover, and cook on a medium-to-low heat for 45-50 minutes, until the chicken is cooked through.

Chicken Kiev

Serves 4

A great classic dish, and one of the most familiar. Kiev is the capital of Ukraine. It was the first capital city of the Russian state, and is called the "mother of Russian cities". This dish tastes truly majestic if freshly prepared at home. The breast is boned and flattened, then stuffed with herbed butter (the garlic was added much later), but the wing bone remains. I always use homemade crisp breadcrumbs (from bread toasted, then crumbed).

4 large chicken breasts, wing bone remaining	*Herb Butter*
salt and pepper	200g (7oz) butter, at room temperature
2 tbsp plain flour	1 tsp each of finely chopped fresh tarragon,
2 eggs, beaten	parsley and chives
6 tbsp homemade breadcrumbs	3 tbsp lemon juice
vegetable oil	

To make the herb butter, place the soft butter, herbs and lemon juice in a small mixing bowl and mix well. Shape the butter into 4 rolls, about 5cm (2 inches) long, and store in the fridge.

Remove the first, thin joint of the wing from each chicken breast and slice the breasts halfway down the middle, using a very sharp knife, to slightly butterfly. Lay each butterflied chicken breast on a work surface and, using a meat hammer, flatten them skin-side down. Season and place a butter roll in the middle of each breast. Roll the breast lengthwise, enclosing the butter and tucking the ends in. Secure with a wooden toothpick.

Put the flour in a shallow bowl, put the beaten eggs in a separate bowl, and put the breadcrumbs in a third bowl.

Roll the breasts in the flour, then dip them in the eggs and coat with the breadcrumbs. Repeat with all the chicken breasts.

Preheat the oil in a deep-fat fryer to a very high temperature (about 180°C/350°F) and fry the chicken pieces 2 at a time for about 8 minutes, until golden brown and cooked through. If you do not have a deep-fat fryer, then you can sauté the fillets in a little oil for 5-6 minutes to brown on all sides, and then place in a preheated oven (180°C/350°F/gas mark 4) for 20 minutes in order to finish cooking.

Beef Stroganoff

Serves 4

The Stroganoff family was dominant for more than five centuries in the Russian aristocracy. This extraordinary family owned a vast palace in St Petersburg, which was strewn with magnificent works of art and antiquities. This dish was created in the late nineteenth century by the French chef to Count Pavel Stroganoff in order to please his employer. Today, beef – or, more properly, *boeuf* – Stroganoff is an international classic, known all over the world and existing in many forms. The essential elements to remember when preparing it are: use the finest fillet of beef you can get, and add some sour cream to a classic mustard sauce. I also add some mushrooms, which is a variation on the classic recipe.

25g (1oz) butter
600g (1lb 5oz) fillet of beef, cut into strips
1 medium onion, peeled and finely chopped
salt and pepper
400g (14oz) wild mushrooms, wiped

1 tbsp cornflour
1 tsp dry mustard powder
200ml (7fl oz) rich beef stock
125ml (4fl oz) sour cream
2 tbsp finely chopped fresh parsley

Heat a large non-stick casserole dish over a medium heat and add half the butter. Sear the meat quickly, stirring all the time, for about 3 minutes. Add the onion and continue cooking for a few more minutes. Season with salt and pepper and transfer to a plate to keep warm.

Add the rest of the butter to the casserole and, when melted, sauté the mushrooms for 5 minutes. Return the beef and onion to the cooking pan, sprinkle with the cornflour and mustard, and stir well. Add the beef stock, continuing to stir, and simmer for 20 minutes.

Add the sour cream and continue cooking on a low heat for a further 5-10 minutes. Stir in the parsley and serve hot. It is usually served with boiled potatoes, but you could offer rice instead.

Hussar's Roast

Serves 6

Hussar's roast is a simple pot roast of beef with horseradish sauce. It is a very popular dish in Lithuania, but the Polish also have their own version. If you are using a boneless roasting joint, the meat can be stuffed with the horseradish, but I prefer to add it to the cooking juices. You can also use veal as I have done here. Serve this dish accompanied by Lithuanian carrot *baba* (*see* page 152).

3 tbsp vegetable oil
1-1.3kg (2lb 4oz-3lb) veal shank
salt and pepper
1 large onion, peeled and finely sliced
1 carrot, scrubbed and finely sliced
2 celery stalks, finely sliced
1 tbsp white-wine vinegar

100ml (3^1/$_2$fl oz) dry white wine
200ml (7fl oz) veal stock
25g (1oz) butter, melted
3 tbsp freshly grated horseradish
3 tbsp fine brioche crumbs
3 tbsp chopped fresh dill

Preheat the oven to 180ºC/350ºF/gas mark 4.

Heat the oil in a large ovenproof dish over a medium heat. Add the meat and brown on all sides. Season with salt and pepper. Take the meat joint out of the dish, and brown the onion, carrot and celery for about 3-4 minutes.

Return the meat to the dish, along with the vinegar, wine and veal stock. Bring to a boil for a couple of minutes, then cover and place in the oven. Cook for 2 hours, or until the meat is tender and coming off the bone easily.

In a small mixing bowl, mix the melted butter, horseradish and brioche crumbs. Take the pot roast out of the oven and stir the horseradish mixture into the juices, then return to the oven for a further 40 minutes.

Slice the meat and serve hot, sprinkled with dill and accompanied by the horseradish sauce and some boiled potatoes.

Veal Skobelev

Serves 4

Mihail Skobelev was one of the finest army officers of his time, becoming a general at the age of 30 after having captured Turkistan for the Russians in 1873. He was a man who lived life to the full, loved great food, good wines and beautiful women, and married a Russian princess. Famous for fighting his battles in a splendid white uniform, which was especially made for him, he rode a white stallion and was known as the "white general". His personal chef created this dish in honour of his victory.

400g (14oz) thin veal escalopes
40g (1¹/2oz) butter
1 large shallot, peeled and finely chopped
400g (14oz) white mushrooms, wiped and
  finely chopped

1 tsp plain flour
125ml (4fl oz) sour cream
125ml (4fl oz) veal stock
60ml (2¹/4fl oz) dry white wine

Ask your butcher to beat the veal escalopes very thin, as he would for a *schnitzel*. Slice them into thin strips.

Heat a third of the butter in a heavy non-stick pan over a medium heat. Add the shallot and sauté until soft, and then add the mushrooms, cooking them until lightly browned. The mushrooms will release some liquid, so cook until this liquid has evaporated. Once cooked, remove from the pan and keep aside until needed.

Melt half of the remaining butter in the same pan and gently sauté the veal strips for 5 minutes.

In a small saucepan, melt the remaining butter and sprinkle in the flour, stirring continuously. Very slowly, add the sour cream and veal stock, again stirring all the time. Continue cooking on a low to medium heat until the sauce has thickened.

Add the shallot and mushroom mixture, the veal and wine, and cook for 10 more minutes. Serve with boiled potatoes.

Nalesniki Pancakes Filled with Sweet Cheese, Nuts and Raisins

Serves 4–6

The Polish version of crêpes or pancakes is called *nalesniki*. They are particularly light and fluffy due to the addition of beaten egg whites. They are usually served with a sweet curd-cheese filling.

200g (7oz) plain flour
$^1/_2$ tsp salt
3 eggs, separated
250ml (9fl oz) milk
250ml (9fl oz) water
2 tbsp vegetable oil
25g (1oz) clarified butter, melted

Filling
200g (7oz) curd cheese
1 tbsp caster sugar
3 tbsp brandy
3 tbsp raisins

Sift the flour and salt together into a large bowl. Make a well in the centre and add the egg yolks. Stir in the milk, water and oil, and mix well to a smooth consistency. Whisk the egg whites to stiff peaks and slowly fold them into the batter.

Place a heavy non-stick pan over a medium heat and, using a pastry brush, brush with some melted clarified butter. When piping hot, pour in a small ladleful of batter and cook on both sides until lightly browned, about a minute on each side. Continue cooking until all the batter is used up – you should make about 8 pancakes, depending on size. Keep the *nalesniki* warm.

To make the filling, place the curd cheese, sugar, brandy and raisins in a bowl and mix together. Spoon some into each pancake and fold them in half and then in half again.

Serve warm or, if desired, place in the oven at 190°C/375°F/gas mark 5 to brown for 10 minutes.

Rich Chocolate Hazelnut Torte

Serves 8–10

This cake is inspired by the rich and delectable *tortes* one can eat in the little Café Ruszwurm in Budapest, easily the best place to have classic Hungarian patisserie. My version is different, but not too different, and can be adapted to become part of your family tradition.

150g (5^1/$_2$oz) butter

200g (7oz) dark chocolate with 70% cocoa solids, chopped

6 large eggs, separated

150g (5^1/$_2$oz) soft brown sugar

2 tbsp plain flour

100g (3^1/$_2$oz) ground hazelnuts

Chocolate Ganache

150ml (5fl oz) double cream

200g (7oz) dark chocolate with 70% cocoa solids, chopped

Hazelnut Topping

150g (5^1/$_2$oz) caster sugar

200g (7oz) shelled hazelnuts, peeled, roasted

Preheat the oven to 180°C/350°F/gas mark 4. Have ready a 20cm (8 inch) round baking tin, buttered and lined with kitchen paper.

Melt the butter very slowly over a low heat. Remove from the heat and add the chopped chocolate, stirring all the time so that it melts in the hot butter. Cool.

Whisk the egg whites to soft peaks, then keep aside until needed.

Whisk the egg yolks and sugar together until thick and pale. Add the chocolate mixture and mix well. Sprinkle in the flour and ground hazelnuts, and mix together carefully. Add the egg whites and fold them in carefully to retain as much air as possible.

Pour into the prepared tin and bake for 25 minutes. The cake should be set, but slightly wobbly in the centre. Cool in the tin.

To prepare the chocolate ganache, heat the cream almost to boiling point. Immediately remove from the heat, and add the chopped chocolate. Stir until all is amalgamated. Cool and then pour over the cake to glaze. Allow to set.

To make the hazelnut topping, place the sugar and 100ml water in a saucepan and cook until lightly caramelized. Remove from the heat and add the whole roasted hazelnuts. Stir briefly to coat. Using tongs, and working quickly, remove the sticky nuts in clusters, and place on lightly oiled baking paper to cool.

Top the cake with hazelnut clusters and serve.

Index

Captions

p9 Wild City Garden, Krakow, Poland; p10 Shlalihidi Market, Tbilisi, Georgia; p11 Antique Market, Budapest, Hungary; p16/17 Images from various markets, Tbilisi, Georgia; p34 Pomegranate tree, Tsodoretti, Georgia; p40/41 Deserdi Market, Tbilisi; p61 Flower Market stall, Tbilisi; p62/63 Milk bar interior, Krakow; p68 Selling peaches at the small market, Mshreta, Georgia; p69 Tinned fruit, Krakow; p83 The Great Hall, Budapest; p84 Clockwise from top left: dry purple basil, fresh paprika, ground paprika and dry Immertian saffron; p90/91 Paprika plants, freshly picked paprika, paprika drying, Kolotcha, Hungary; p105/106 Walnuts and plums at Deserdi Market, Tbilisi; p107 Favourite plum snacks, Deserdi Market, Tbilisi; p114 Clockwise from top left: mulberries, beans, gooseberries and beets, Rustavi, Georgia; p115 Wild mushrooms, street sellers, Georgia; p125 Flour stall, Covered market, Tbilisi; p136/137 Bread-making and bread, near Riva Kura, Tbilisi; p147 Cheese shop, near Central Market, Tbilisi, Georgia; p148/149 Street market sellers, including hand made cheese, Krakow, Poland; p157 Ostipki home-made cheese, Zakopane, Poland; p160/161 Farmed animals, Tsodoretti, Georgia; p163 Khachapuri, Tsodoretti, Georgia; p169 The Gundel Restaurant, Budapest, Hungary; p170 Typical architecture, Krakow, Poland; p171 Cafe at a market stall, Tbilisi; p176 Front gates, clockwise from top left: Tbilisi, Krakow and Budapest; p177 Krakow, Poland.

Bibliography

A Taste of Russia, Darra Goldstein (Robert Hale, London, 1985); *A Year of Russian Feasts*, Catherine Chermeteff Jones (Jellyroll Press, 2002); *The Bacillus of Long Life*, Loudon M Douglas (GP Putman's Sons, New York, 1911); *The Balkan Cookbook*, Inge Kramarz (Crown, New York, 1972); *The Best of Ukrainian Cuisine*, Bohdan Zahny (Hippocrene Books, 1994); *Cooking with Yogurt*, Ifran Orga (Andre Deutsch, 1956); *The Cuisine of Hungary*, George Lang (Bonanaza Books, New York, 1971); *Cuisines of Caucasus Mountains*, Kay Shaw Nelson (Hippocrene Books, New York, 2002); *Eat Russian*, Sofka Skipwith (David & Charles, Devon, 1973); *Eating the Russian Way*, Beryl Gould-Marks (Gramercy, New York, 1967); *Ethnographic Journey about Georgia*, Otar Miminoshoili (Tbilisi, 1988); *Food and Drink in Medieval Poland*, Maria Dembinska (Pennsylvania Press Philadelphia, 1999); *Food of Eastern Europe*, Lesley Chamberlain (Lorenz Books, New York, 2002); *Georgian Cuisine*, Tamar Lomidze (Tbilisi, 2004); *Georgian Culture*, Rusudan Tsurtsumia (Kandelaki's Foundation, 1999); *Georgian Dishes*, Sakartvelos Matsne (Tbilisi, 2002); *The Georgian Feast*, Darra Goldstein (University of California Press, Berkeley, 1999); *Good Food*, Meirel Buchanan (Frederick Muller Ltd, London, 1956); *Gotvarska Kniga*, Genadi Spasov (B Zilber, 1895); *The Hungarian Cookbook*, Susan Derecskey (Harper Perennial, 1987); *Hungarian Cookery*, Lilla Deeley (The Medici Society Ltd, London, 1968); *Hungarian Cookery Book*, Karoly Gundel (Corvina Press, Budapest, 1965); *Hungarian Cuisine*, Mariska Vizvari (Corvina, Szeged, 1994); *Katish, Our Russian Cook*, Wanda L Frolov (The Modern Library, New York, 2001); *Latviiska Kuhnia*, Irina Grebovnaia (Riga, 1988); *Little Odessa Flavours,* Sergei Volostov (New York, 1964); *The Melting Pot*, Maria Kaneva-Johnson (Prospect Books, Devon, 1999); *New Hungarian Cookbook*, Kalman Kalla Gundel (Pallas Studio, Budapest, 1998); *Nothing Beets Borscht*, Jane Blanksteen (Atheneum, New York, 1974); *Old Polish Traditions*, Maria Lemnis and Henyk Vitry (Warsaw, 1848); *Please to the Table*, Anya von Bremzen and John Welchman (Workman, New York, 1990); *Polish Heritage Cookery*, Robert & Maria Strybel (Hippocrene Books, 1993); *The Polish Kitchen*, Mary Pininska (Grub Street, London, 2000); *Recipes from Hungary*, Evelin Bach (The Shenval Press, London, 1938); *Ruskaia Kuhnia*, Cath Reddiford (Help Russia's Elderly, London, 1971); *Russia as Seen and Described by Famous Writers*, edited by Esther Singleton (Dodd, Mead and Co, New York, 1904); *Russian Cooking*, Helen and George Papashvily (Time Life, Long Books, Virginia, 1969); *Russian Food and Drink*, Valentina Lapenkova (The Bookwright Press, New York, 1988); *Russian Jew Cooks in Peru*, Violeta Authumn (101 Productions, San Francisco, 1973); *Suvremenna Domashna Kuhnia*, Penka Cholcheva and Tzvetana Kalaidgieva (Tehnika, Sofia, 1972).

Footnotes

1. Page 6: from a nameless poem by Aleksey Konstantinovich Tolstoy, from *Polnoe Sobranie Stickhotvorenia (Complete Collected Poems – Volume 1)*, page 284, published in St Petersburg, 1888. Translation by Silvena Rowe.

2. Page 8: Sobolka Fire by John Kochanowski, from *Specimens of the Polish Poets*, compiled and translated by John Bowring, 1827.

3. Page 32: Pomegranates by Malcolm J Rowe, 2006.

4. Page 60: Ode for Music on St Cecilia's Day by Alexander Pope, from *Poetical Works – 2 volumes*, published by James Nichol, 1856.

5. Page 82: Pan Tadeusz by Adam Mickiewicz, published by Lwow; Wydawn, Zakladu Narodowego Imienia Ossolonkich, 1921. Translation by Silvena Rowe.

6. Page 104: Eugene Onegin, a novel in verse, by Alexander Pushkin, from *Polnoe Sobranie Sochinenii v Shesti Tomakh Pod Obshchei Redaktsiei (Complete Collected Works in 6 Tomes Under Collective Editing Work),* volume 4, printed in Moskva, published by Gos. Izd-vo Khudozhestvnnoi Lit-ry 1930–31. Translation by Silvena Rowe.

7. Page 124: The Nights in the Village near Dikanka by NB Gogol, from *Polnoe Sobranie Sochinenii (Complete Collected Works) volume 1,* published by Leipzig Franz Wagner, 1836. Translation by Silvena Rowe.

8. Page 146: Eugene Onegin, a novel in verse, by Alexander Pushkin (as above).

9. Page 168: Eugene Onegin, a novel in verse, by Alexander Pushkin (as above).

Thanks

Most of all, thanks to Grainne Fox at Ed Victor's, who is so much more than a literary agent to me; to Jonathan Lovekin for making this book so gorgeous and in the process becoming a great friend; and to the one-and-only Caz Hildebrand for saying yes. Without Nicola Collings' and Tim Foster's vision and attention this book would not be, so thanks for being on my side. Thanks to Becca Spry, my editor at Mitchell Beazley, and to the best of the best, Susan Fleming. I must also express my gratitude to Robert Kusy, as well as to Balazs Szucs and Elizabeth Courage from the Hungarian National Tourist Office, London. Not forgetting my dear friend John Woroniecki, whose knowledge and passion for all things East European have fuelled my own.